Order Out of Chaos

by

Dr. Leon Stutzman

Order Out of Chaos

by

Dr. Leon Stutzman

Vincom, Inc.
Tulsa, Oklahoma

Unless otherwise indicated, all Scripture quotations are taken from the *King James Version of the Bible*.

Order Out of Chaos
ISBN 0-927936-74-7
Copyright © 1995 by
Dr. Leon Stutzman
P. O. Box 1164
Dayton, OH 45401

Published by Vincom, Inc.
P. O. Box 702400
Tulsa, OK 74170
(918) 254-1276

Dedication

Thanks to everyone on my staff for their diligent efforts, especially Evelyn Malone and Angie Williams.

This book is especially dedicated to the woman of God, my wife of twenty some years, Connie, who helps bring order out of chaos.

Contents

1

Out of Order

One day, a hitchhiker was walking down the road, and a car pulled up beside him. The driver of the car stopped and told the hitchhiker to jump in. Grateful for the ride, the hitchhiker hopped into the car. The speed of the car quickly soared to 90 miles per hour as the driver stepped on the accelerator, pressing it to the floor, wheels spinning.

When the driver came to a red light, instead of stopping, he looked both ways and raced right through it.

"Man, you're going to get us killed!" screamed the hitchhiker in terror.

"Don't worry, my brother taught me to drive," the driver calmly responded, and continued down the road driving 90 miles per hour.

Soon, they came to another red light. Again, the driver glanced both ways and zipped through the red light, narrowly missing another car. The hitchhiker was more horrified than before.

"Man, you're going to get us killed!" he yelled.

Again, the driver calmly responded, "Don't worry, my brother taught me to drive."

They continued down the road going 90 miles per hour, and they came to a green light. The driver stomped on the brake and brought the car to a screeching halt.

The hitchhiker shrieked, "Man, you're crazy!"

The driver said, "My brother uses this road."

Unlike the driver, most people stop at red lights and drive through green lights.

Can you imagine what the roads would be like if half of the vehicles stopped at red lights and half stopped at green lights?

Can you imagine what the roads would be like if half of the people drove on red lights and half of the people drove on green lights?

Society needs a certain amount of order to function. Early in 1994, an American teenager living temporarily in Singapore, was arrested for allegedly vandalizing cars and stealing street signs. The punishment for committing any crime in Singapore is quite severe compared to American standards.

When he was found guilty, the young man received four lashes with a rattan cane. The Singapore police actually dropped that penalty from six lashes, four months in prison, and a $2,200 fine after a call from President Clinton.

It may seem that the laws and punishments are extreme in the Republic of Singapore, but since 1965, Singapore has gone from being a backward province of Malaysia to become one of the super powers of Asia. This independent nation, about three times the size of Washington, DC, is not a democracy, but a republic within a commonwealth.[1]

Lee Kuan Yew, prime minister since 1965 and leader of the party that brought independence, along with other leaders, determined that Singapore would remain a clean, safe, beautiful city and nation. They paid attention to even the smallest details, things that cause a place to look trashy, such as gum stuck under park benches.

There would be no chewing gum spit out on the streets at all, they decided. The only way to assure this was not to have a great many trash collectors as we would do in the states, but to make it illegal to chew gum in public!

Most Westerners think Singapore laws are too harsh and the penalties are unreasonable or even cruel. A Dutch man was hanged in the fall of 1994 for trying to smuggle heroin into Singapore. However, the city is said to have the safest streets on earth. A visitor or resident of that Oriental city does not have to worry about getting mugged, having a purse or wallet stolen, or any of the other crimes Americans take for granted as everyday concerns.

Citizens of the tiny state did not think the young man's punishment too great. They were concerned about those who had to get their cars repaired and taxpayers who had to pay for new signs.

One Singapore mother of teenagers said, "I would be ashamed if my son did anything like that. It would mean that I hadn't raised him properly."[2]

Many people also seem to have no idea that, when visiting a foreign country, they must subject themselves to the order of that country.

A visitor to Singapore or any other foreign place, cannot say, "I am an American citizen. I can do here what I do in the United States."

That person might find himself in a deep, dark, dank dungeon. The concept of human rights in a foreign country may be different from our concept of human rights. Their concept might be society's right to a gum-free, crime-free, clean city at the expense of a certain amount of individual freedom.

One of the problems in our society of "independence" and freedom of action is that many times there is a lack of order. There are too many people running through red lights and stopping on green lights, figuratively speaking. This is the kind of chaos that can be dangerous.

The Bible teaches a lot about chaos and order. In fact, the entire book, God's plan for mankind and the earth, is about bringing His order out of the chaos resulting from rebellion and disobedience.

The Biblical Origin of Chaos

If a sign were to be hung in space on the planet earth, it would read "Out of Order."

Perhaps you have heard of "Murphy's Law." This somewhat facetious "law" states that if anything can go wrong, it will go wrong at the worst possible moment.

Have you ever felt that you were a victim of Murphy's Law?

Have you ever thought everything was going along nicely when suddenly chaos entered in, and everything that could go wrong did go wrong at the worst possible moment?

Chaos is the absence of order.

There is a powerful truth in the first few verses of Genesis. Remember that Genesis is "the book of beginnings."

> In the beginning God created the heaven and the earth.
>
> And the earth was without form, and void; and darkness was upon the face of the deep. And the Spirit of God moved upon the face of the waters.
>
> And God said, Let there be light: and there was light.
>
> **Genesis 1:1-3**

In the beginning, God created the heavens and the earth. And as God is a God Who desires things to be done "decently and in order" (1 Cor. 14:40) and who does all things perfectly, we know He could not have created the earth "without form and void."

Two Hebrew words are used in Genesis 1:2: *tohuw* (tohoo) and *bohuw* (bohoo),[3] which together, in essence convey the idea of "chaotic." The first word means, among other things, "to lie waste, confusion, wilderness, empty place." The second word means "an undistinguishable ruin, emptiness, void." Therefore, between verses 1 and 2 of Genesis, the heavens and the earth, created perfect, had somehow become chaotic.

We get a glimpse of what must have happened in only a few places in the Bible. In Isaiah 14:4-17, we read of the rebellion that took place in heaven when God cast out Lucifer, the son of the morning, known to us as Satan, or the devil.

The "accuser of the brethren," another name for this fallen being, and one-third of the angels, were cast out of God's heaven, and caused the earth to become chaotic and empty in the process. Although Satan was created perfect by God (Ezek. 28:15), through his iniquity and fall, chaos entered the universe.

Talking of Lucifer, God said:

> . . . That made the world as a wilderness, and
> destroyed the cities thereof. . . .
>
> Isaiah 14:17

Chaos originated in rebellion against God. And out of that chaos, God began the work of re-creation, outlined in Genesis 1:2-31. God brought order out of chaos. God always brings order out of chaos. God is the only One Who can bring order out of chaos, even the chaos of your life.

Where there was chaos, God brought order. In the first fifteen verses in the book of Genesis, every time God speaks, something comes into an ordered existence. Genesis 2:1 states:

> Thus the heavens and the earth were finished,
> and all the host of them.

And Genesis 1:31 says that God saw everything He had made, and it was very good. Chaos had been sub-dued by order. The re-creation was done. God brought order out of chaos, but His perfect earth did not last. In Genesis 2:8, we read:

> And the Lord God planted a garden eastward in
> Eden; and there he put the man whom he had formed.

Eden means "pleasure" or "delicate, delight,"[4] This pleasure garden of God was Adam's dominion and Eve's domicile. The Garden of Eden was where God put mankind and set forth His first commands, in Gen-esis 1:28:

> Be fruitful, and multiply, and replenish the
> earth, and subdue it.

Why did God assign them work to do in the midst of this perfection? He did this first of all because order must be maintained. Also, God knew that man must work to be truly satisfied and fulfilled.

God Himself "worked" six days and rested one. He created man to be about *His* work, and He created a perfect planet. However, He left work for man to do in keeping His world orderly. Nature will not "order" itself, contrary to the theories of evolutionists. Mankind was to be God's sons and partners in maintaining order in nature as well as in society.

When Adam and Eve disobeyed God and got in agreement with Satan, the father of chaos, they were cast out of the pleasant garden. (Gen. 3.) Adam and Eve had chosen chaos over order, rebellion over obedience, so they could not stay there.

For their own good, they then had to take dominion, replenish, and subdue the earth the hard way — by the sweat of their brows. (Gen. 3:17,19,22,23.)

The result of their sin is that chaos became the natural order of the planet, although the earth never again became "without form and void" as it had after Satan's rebellion. Even the flood of Noah's time did not bring utter chaos again. It only cleansed the earth of every living thing except Noah's family and the animals in the ark. The ark itself was representative of God's order.

Before the flood, the earth was on the verge once again of total chaos (Gen. 6:12,13), which is why God brought the flood — to give His re-created planet another chance. God's aim always is "order out of chaos."

The Earth Is "Out of Order"

People without God live in a chaotic society and chaotic cultures, no matter how orderly they seem in the natural. That is because only the spiritual realm of God's Kingdom remains perfectly in order today. The

United States, which for almost two hundred years walked predominately according to God's order, is reflecting today the chaos that crept into our thinking and society during the latter part of this century.

When we become born again, God calls us, as new creatures in Christ Jesus and empowered by the Holy Spirit, to "subdue" the chaotic areas of our lives. That is the only assignment God gave Adam and Eve. Genesis 2:15 says:

> **And the Lord God took the man, and put him into the garden of Eden to dress it and to keep it.**

The earth is in a chaotic state, and Adam and Eve became part of the chaos when they allowed themselves to be influenced by Satan. Too often, the people of God are influenced by what goes on around them, instead of being influenced and led by the Spirit of God.

Before you became a Christian, you were in a chaotic state, ruled by the principalities and the powers of this world, Satan's cohorts. (Col. 2:15.) However, you became "a new creature" (2 Cor. 5:17) when you accepted Jesus as your personal Savior. However, there may still be chaotic areas in your soul and body that have to be subdued.

When Bible scholars say that people are "free moral agents," they mean God not only created man with the ability to make choices and decisions, but He gave us the *right to choose*. You have a right to choose, but if you make the wrong choices, you are liable to the consequences of those choices.

> **Whatsoever a man soweth, that shall he also reap.**
>
> **Galatians 6:7**

One of the saddest funerals I ever conducted was for a man whom I had grown to love. He had been saved while watching Christian television. After he had been in our services a few weeks, he made a personal appointment with me to ask if he would be welcome in our church with his previous background.

He had been a practicing homosexual, involved in the "gay fast-lane" lifestyle of the New York bathhouses. I assured him that he certainly was welcome in our church. When he was born again, God delivered him from his chaotic condition and set him free from the bondage of homosexuality.

We came to know him well and enjoyed watching him praise the Lord. He wore one of the worst hair pieces I have ever seen. Sometimes he would leap into the air as he worshipped, and his toupee would keep right on going. Three or four inches of air would show between it and his head. He enjoyed the Lord, and we enjoyed him.

However, the consequences of chaos caught up with him, and he died with a rare AIDS-related cancer. Chaos always has an end result of destruction. His spirit was saved and went home to be with the Lord, but his body was subject to the result of chaos.

Although God forgave him and delivered him, he never fully dealt with one issue concerning his former lifestyle. He never told his former lover that he had been born again and had forsaken the gay lifestyle. This other man lives in an Ohio city, is married with three children, and does not even know that his "friend" died with AIDS. More than likely, his wife knows nothing of this part of her husband's life. This is only one aspect of the chaos our society has allowed in sexual matters.

It is true that each person has the right to make their choices in life. God gave us the right. But, you can make the wrong choice as Adam and Eve discovered, as Aaron's sons Abihu and Nadab discovered, and as many others in the Bible discovered. The world is out of order, and yet, God is a God of order.

God Instilled Order in Israel

I love reading the Old Testament, because as I read, I get a sense of God's order. When Israel camped round about the tabernacle, every tribe camped in its assigned spot. People rallied around the banner of their tribes.

One tribe did not say, "Well, we think we're going to move on the other side of the tabernacle this week because we're tired of being on the east side of the tabernacle. We're going to move to the west side."

The people in the tribes on the south side of the tabernacle did not say, "We're tired of being the south-side Israelites. We've decided to become north-side Israelites. And we're going to move our place around the tabernacle."

No one decided what his or her place would be around the tabernacle. It was assigned by God through Moses. Throughout the Old Testament, we can see how God brought order into the lives of His people.

And one thing God wants to do in your life is to bring order, so that you can defeat the chaos that surrounds you. You must "subdue the earth" in order to be everything God has called you to be and to have everything He has called you to have.

You see, God is a God of order. I like Exodus 40:4:

> **And thou shalt bring in the table, and set in order the things that are to be set in order upon it . . . .**

The word *order* is used twice in that verse. In fact, God spoke the words "in order" fourteen times to Moses during the time when he was setting the people of Israel in order as a nation. For example, the priests were to set in order the things that were to be upon the Table of Shewbread. Exodus 40:4 goes on to say, . . . **thou shall bring in the candlestick, and light the lamps thereof.**

Do you know there is no revelation without order?

Three words explain what killed the Charismatic movement: revelation without order. There was a lot of good teaching, but very little order. You cannot have the "lamp" lit until the "Table of Shewbread" (literally "table of His presence")[5] is first put in order.

The "shew" bread (twelve cakes, or loaves, of bread) to be placed on the table were a type of Jesus, one for each tribe, encompassing all Israel. In the New Testament, the twelve disciples encompassed the Church. (Rev. 21:12-14.) Jesus specifically said that He was the "Bread of Life." (John 6:35,51.) For us to even receive revelation or illumination, we must be set in order. We must be "feeding" on the bread, "in order."

If the lamp is lit before there is order concerning the Bread, you are apt "to go off in all directions," instead of moving in the Lord's direction. Order (maintaining the Christian walk) has to precede revelation in your life.

A New Testament text along this line is Ephesians 1:17:

> **That the God of our Lord Jesus Christ, the Father of glory, may give unto you the spirit of wisdom and revelation in the knowledge of him.**

First Corinthians 15 is another powerful scripture passage along this line. The most miserable person in the world is the person who tries to get out of his/her order and into another person's order.

But every man in his own order: Christ the firstfruits; afterward they that are Christ's at his coming.

Then cometh the end, when he shall have delivered up the kingdom to God, even the Father; when he shall have put down all rule and all authority and power.

. . . . that God may be all in all.

Verses 23,24,28

Even Jesus walked in order, and if Jesus walked in order, and we are to follow Him (Matt. 16:24), we ought to walk in order.

Endnotes

[1] Wright, John W. Gen. Ed., *The Universal Almanac* (Kansas City: Andrews & McMeel, 1990, p. 478.

[2] Bordewich, Fergus M. "The Country That Works Perfectly," *Reader's Digest*, (Pleasantville, NY: Reader's Digest Association, Inc.), Vol. 146, # 874, February, 1995, p. 104.

[3] Strong, James. *The New Strong's Exhaustive Concordance of the Bible* (Nashville: Thomas Nelson Pub., 1990), "Hebrew and Chaldee Dictionary," p. 123, #8414, and p. 19, #922.

[4] *Ibid.*, p. 85, #5730.

[5] Ness, Alex W. *Pattern for Living* (Downsview, Ontario, Canada: Christian Centre Publications, 1979), pp. 107-109.

2

Opting for Order

There is a connection between order and steadfastness in faith. Read Colossians 2:5:

> **For though I be absent in the flesh, yet am I with you in the spirit, joying and beholding your order, and the stedfastness of your faith in Christ.**

You can never help some people because their lives are too filled with chaos. One example is a man whom I spent a lot of time dealing with, working with, and trying to help. God intervened supernaturally in the man's life many times.

He came into my church sick and afflicted in his body. As a commercial airline pilot, he had taken the wrong medication while flying an aircraft. When he became a Christian, he felt that to really repent, he could never fly again. He returned all of his flying papers to the Federal Aviation Administration (FAA). Still sick in his body and still requiring the medication which prohibited him from flying, he came into the church.

God gave me a word of knowledge for him. God healed him, so that he did not need the medication any longer. When he wrote to the FAA to inquire about his status, they said all that was necessary was for them to send him duplicates of his credentials. He could go back to flying the next day.

God moved supernaturally in his life, healed him, delivered him, yet he still ended up living on the streets because his life was filled with chaos.

Another example of a person with a chaotic life is a homeless man we brought into the church and gave a job. The church provided for him, fed him, and clothed him. He was taken off the streets and placed in a temporary shelter. Eventually, he got his own home.

One day, I said, "You know, you're in a real position to help other people who are in the same situation you were in."

His answer was that he did not want to have anything to do with "those homeless people." Two weeks later, one of my pastors talked to him about a job he was supposed to do around the church.

The man said, "You can't talk to me that way. I quit."

After all the caring, time, energy, and money the church staff and members spent on him, he quit. And where did he end up? Back on the streets. He was not what would be thought of as "a bad person," just chaotic. The pilot was also a wonderful person. Both men had lives filled with chaos.

Read Colossians 2:5 again:

> **For though I be absent in the flesh, yet am I with you in the spirit, joying and beholding your order, and the stedfastness of your faith in Christ.**

Why are so many folks up one day and down the next? They are in the church; they are out. They are not stable, they are not strong, because they are chaotic. They live in chaos, from crisis to crisis, with no order at all. You can live in chaos and confusion, or you can opt for order.

There was a time when my life was very chaotic, but I thought I was being led by the Spirit of God. Today, I have opted to live in order and have discovered that I like order much better than chaos.

Areas That Might Be Changed

Here are a few areas you might want to consider applying this truth about order to:

1. *Your head.*

In Joshua 2:6, Rahab brought the two unnamed spies to the roof of the house, and hid them with the stalks of flax, which she had laid in order upon the roof. All through Scripture, flax represents humanity. It represents who you are as a human being. Rahab hid the two witnesses in the flax that was "laid in order" upon the roof. Those two spies, who represented the Word and the Spirit, were placed in stalks of flax laid out in an orderly fashion. When you allow God to order your thinking by the Word and the Spirit, the Word of God becomes effective in your life. You need to order your thinking.

2. *Your home.*

In Judges 13:12, a man of the tribe of Dan spoke these words to the angel who brought news of a son to be born to him and his wife:

> . . . Now let thy words come to pass. How shall we order the child, and how shall we do unto him?

Who is in charge at your house?

Perhaps I could be called "old-fashioned." When I go to a shopping mall and see a four-year-old lying in the floor, kicking and screaming because he or she cannot have the latest incarnation of the newest television fad, I want to spank the parent, not the child. There is nothing wrong with most children that a little bit of order will not cure.

If you instill order into your child's life when he/she is young, you would not have trouble with the child later. Of course, every teenager is going to test the bounds of order, that is what teenage years are all about.

My wife and I have three teenagers, and I can testify that they are good children. However, that does not mean they are perfect kids. They are totally involved in "Standard Teenage Stupid Stuff" (SASS). Think about when you were a teenager. Did you do some stupid stuff?

Ever so often a parent will come to me and say, "Pastor, my child has done thus-and-so, what should I do about it?"

I say, "Nothing," then I ask, "Did you raise him right?"

"Yeah."

"Did you put the Word of God in him?"

"Yeah."

"Pray for him?"

"Yeah."

"Then he is just operating in 'standard teenage stupid stuff.' "

All you have to do is to remind your child who is in charge. By the way, parents are *supposed* to be in charge. And if you cannot base this on biblical reasons, such as **Honour thy father and thy mother** (Ex. 20:12a), I will give you a practical reason: Parents pay the bills! Society has too many chaotic homes.

3. *God's House*

In 2 Chronicles 29:35, we see:

> And also the burnt offerings were in abundance, with the fat of the peace offerings, and the drink offerings for every burnt offering. So the service of the house of the Lord was set in order.

Going to church is more than a Sunday morning celebration meeting. It is about service, about being involved in other people's lives. It is about being involved in the community. When you come into order, you are going to be involved. That does not mean that every moment of your waking day is going to be taken up with the church.

I have friends whom I love, who are trying to establish order by having something going on every day at their churches. Some people think they have to be in every activity to be a good church member. No one has to be involved in everything.

However, a church member should be involved in something beyond going to church on Sunday morning, if for no other reason than building relationships within the family of God. Also, you will be blessed and benefit by whatever good you sow into other people's lives. Blessings will come upon your house as it is set in order.

Not every Israelite functioned in the order of God, however. Leviticus 10:1 states that Aaron's two oldest sons, Nadab and Abihu, chose to initiate their priestly duties in their own order, not God's. The consequence was destruction.

> And Nadab and Abihu, the sons of Aaron, took either of them his censer, and put fire therein, and put incense thereon, and offered strange fire before the Lord, which he commanded them not.

They were about their priestly duties and believed they could carry out those duties according to their own order. Their way of doing things, however, was not the way God told them to do it. Certainly, their hearts and motives reflected chaos and not God's order.

Leviticus 10:2 continues:

> And there went out fire from the Lord, and devoured them, and they died before the Lord.

Nadab and Elihu burned to death and died in front of Moses, because they were *out of the prescribed order*. Aaron's sons had a choice: God's way or their own way, just as Adam and Eve did, just as we do.

4. *Your present*

Psalm 50:23 says:

> Whoso offereth praise glorifieth me: and to him that ordereth his conversation aright will I shew the salvation of God.

As well as your behavior and activities, you also must order your conversation. Acts 11:26 tells us the disciples were first called Christians at Antioch.

Antioch was a great city, and the church there was a cosmopolitan group made up of people from many different walks of life and many different social and economic backgrounds.

Yet, when the Antiochians saw the people in the church there, they said, "These people are all different, but they all exhibit the characteristics of Christ."

And, although the term was first used as a derogatory and rather sarcastic description ("little Christs"), it soon became an honored term for the followers of Jesus, who had called themselves "Nazarenes" or "followers of the Way" until then.[1]

Being a Christian means that, when you leave the church building and someone cuts you off in the parking lot, you do not do what you would have before you became a Christian. Philippians 3:20 says:

> **For our conversation is in heaven; from whence also we look for the Saviour, the Lord Jesus Christ.**

If you are a Christian, act like a Christian. Be a Christian. And if you have a hard time being a Christian, you need to deal with the chaos in your life and bring yourself into order. It is not tough to be a Christian if you have order in your life.

If you go to church with a hangover or sit at home watching a television ministry because you have a hangover, your life is out of order.

If you are married and looking at someone else's husband or wife, you are out of order. You need to deal with the chaos in your life and let the order of God take over.

5. *Your future*

David, king and psalmist of Israel, knew about order and knew that it is an integral part of the life of a child of God. Psalm 119:133 says:

> **Order my steps in thy word: and let not any iniquity have dominion over me.**

Psalm 37:23 says, **The steps of a good man are ordered by the Lord.**

God orders our steps when we allow Him to order them. Remember, God made you a "free moral agent." He gave you the right to choose. You can chose to go your own way, do your own thing, or you can allow God to order your steps.

If you allow God to order your steps, He will always order them in the direction of what is best for you. It may not appear that what He has ordained is the best for you when you are walking in those steps, but hindsight will show you every time that He was right. I am speaking from personal experience when I say that, when God orders your steps, He orders your steps for His good and your good.

The steps of a good man are ordered of the Lord, and the steps of a good woman are ordered of the Lord, and he or she delights in His way. David understood the necessity of having a life that is ordered by God.

Four Revelations About Order

If you get a revelation in your heart of the following four concepts, they will change your thinking, which will change your behavior:

*The absence of order is chaos. That is what chaos is all about — the lack of order. Judges 21:25 tells us of a time in Israel after Moses and before Samuel when there was no consistent order in the nation.

> **In those days there was no king in Israel: every man did that which was right in his own eyes.**

Does that describe a society which sounds familiar to us today?

Does that describe the "Me Generation"?

There was as yet no king in Israel, and because there was no king, there was no order, except for the fifteen times when things got so out of hand that God raised up a judge to exercise some authority over the chaos in society. So every man did "that which is right in his own eyes" for most of that four-hundred-year period.

It might surprise many of the people who know me now that, before I became a Christian in my teenage years, I was an "anarchist." An anarchist is someone who does not believe there should be any laws, but that everyone should be able to do whatever he or she wants to as long as no one gets hurt. And some do not even care whether someone gets hurt.

One day in English class, I was assigned to write on anything I wanted to write about. I was an anarchist, so I wrote this wonderful "anarchist manifesto." It was great. I got a "B" on the paper, but only after the teacher called me into his office and talked to me for a half-hour about the error of my thinking.

After I became a Christian I discovered that, if you are not a hermit on a mountain and are living in society, you have responsibilities:

If you are a father, you have responsibilities.

If you are a mother, you have responsibilities.

If you are an employer, you have responsibilities.

If you are an employee, you have responsibilities.

Because you are in the middle of society, you have civic and social responsibilities.

The absence of order is chaos. People do whatever is right in their own eyes; therefore, chaos is a natural state. Chaos is the absence of order. If you have no order in your life, your life is disintegrating right now. You may not know it, but your life *is* disintegrating right now.

Why do bodies die? Because bodies operate in chaotic conditions. Many people are setting themselves up for major problems because they love anything that contains cholesterol. Breakfast is a cup of caffeine-loaded coffee, or a carbonated, caffeine-loaded soft drink and a "moon pie." For lunch, there may be another soft drink and some fast food or a fat-loaded snack. Then they go home at night and have TV dinners or more fast food.

Christians who maintain this kind of diet keep saying they do not understand why they feel so badly. I do. Their biggest exercise is taking a remote control and clicking through the channels. They have enormously large thumb muscles because that is the only muscle that is toned.Would your thumb muscle be a prejudicial testament to your favorite form of activity — lying in a recliner, flipping from channel to channel to channel?

If so, ten years from now, you may be calling your pastor to ask for prayer because you have hypertension, heart palpitations, stomach ulcers, or some other sickness in your body.

If you were to hear from heaven, you probably would hear God say, "Get your body in order, and you will not have most of those problems."

I am not advocating a macrobiotic diet of all rice or anything else fanatical. I love steak, and I eat it. All I am saying is that we need to develop orderly lifestyles for good health as well as for a victorious Christian walk. And eating properly, exercising enough, and getting enough rest is all part of an orderly lifestyle.

*Order can cause chaos, but chaos never causes order. If you do not believe it, try to get your teenagers in order. That will cause some chaos.

In Genesis 11:9, we read that some of Noah's descendants were building a tower called Babel, and God came down and confused them. Order caused chaos. Order can cause chaos because of free moral agency. If you do not submit to order, you are causing chaos.

If you do not submit to the order of a church, you will cause chaos in the church. And if there is a sufficient number of other chaotic people in the church, chaos results in dissension. But if everyone else is walking in order, they can immediately spot chaos in you. The fire that fell on Aaron's sons fell because they were out of order, and that order rewarded chaos with destruction.

*Order has its own inherent power. Daniel 14:17 is a powerful passage of scripture. You should also read Daniel 4 about Nebuchadnezzar, the king of Babylon, who saw God deliver the three Hebrews out of the fiery furnace. He knew their God was "a" god, but he did not know that their God was *the* God.

Everything was going along well in his life. By the way, Nebuchadnezzar means "protected by Nebo" and Nebo was the Babylonian god of understanding and wisdom. So, essentially, he was supposed to be protected by understanding and wisdom, but he did not have understanding and wisdom. His life was out of order.

He dreamed about a tree being cut down and seven years later being resurrected or regrown, and he wanted to know what the dream meant. Daniel gave him the interpretation. He told Nebuchadnezzar that God was going to take the kingdom away from him for seven years. But afterwards, his kingdom would be restored.

Well, it all transpired as Daniel had prophesied and predicted. Having wandered as a beast of the field for seven years, his memory and his mind suddenly came back to him.

His response was not, "God, why did You cause that to happen in my life?" Or, "God, it was not fair to take seven years out of my life!"

His response was, "God, *You're* God, and from now on I am going to worship You. I am going to acknowledge You. I am going to walk in order from this time on."

Order *does* have its own inherent power. When your steps are ordered by God, you walk in that power. From the natural perspective, there is power in order. You get more things done when your life is in order.

*Order can kill those who live in chaos. Aaron's sons were killed because of their rebellion. God sent fire out of heaven and killed them. Do you think Moses sympathized with his brother, Aaron? No, Moses was an ordered man. He looked at Aaron and, in fact, you will find that Moses warned Aaron and the Israelites not to show mourning for people who merited God's judgment. (Lev. 10:6,7.)

> **Then Moses said unto Aaron, This is it that the Lord spake, saying, I will be sanctified in them that come nigh me, and before all the people I will be glorified. And Aaron held his peace.**
>
> **Leviticus 10:3**

Although Nadab and Abihu may have been "good" men in other ways, the chaos in their thinking killed them. *Nadab* means "liberal," and *Abihu* means "worshipper of God."[2] Nadab was a liberal man, and Abihu was a worshipper. However, they offered up "strange fire," incense not according to God's order. Chaos kills!

Leviticus 10:4 tells us what else happened.

> **And Moses called Mishael and Elzaphan, the sons of Uzziel the uncle of Aaron, and said unto them, Come near, carry your brethren from before the sanctuary out of the camp.**

Mishael means "who (is) what God (is)."[3] If you want to order your steps, the first thing is to understand that you belong to God. You are not your own. You were bought with a price. (1 Cor. 6:20.) That is why God said to glorify Him in your body which is Christ's.

Read Psalm 50:23 again. It says:

> . . . to him that ordereth his conversation aright will I shew the salvation of God.

If you will order your conversation, God will not have to.

If you order your life, God will not have to.

Do you know God is good in the middle of your chaos?

Leviticus 10:5 says some men "went near" and carried Nadab and Abihu out of the camp in their coats. The "coats" they were wearing were the robes of their priesthood. The chaotic condition of their lives caused them to be killed. God did not say He was blotting their names out of the Book. They were carried out in their priesthood. John 1:17 says:

> For the law was given by Moses, but grace and truth came by Jesus Christ.

In spite of the chaos in our lives, God often continues to bless us. However, His best for us is to take the chaos out of our lives, because chaos eventually will destroy us. I close this chapter with one two-sided thought:

If you order your steps, you will be blessed. If you walk in chaos, chaos will cause the curse to come. The choice is yours.

Endnotes

[1] Comay, Joan. *Who's Who in the Old Testament* (Nashville: Abingdon. Press, 1971), pp. 464,205.

[2] *Strong's*, p. 76, #5070; p. 7, #30.

[3] *Ibid.*, p. 65, #4332.

3

Ten Steps Out of Chaos

In the last chapter, we found that there are two forces at work in the world today: chaos and order. Perhaps you know someone who is living in a chaotic condition. Perhaps that someone is you.

A chaotic condition can also be described as Christless-living. Chaotic living is when the only consistency in your life is inconsistency. You never know what you are going to do from one day to the next day. You have no clear-cut plans, purposes, or goals. You float through life, living from one crisis to the next. You die and your epitaph reads, "He died and nobody noticed."

Most Christians will agree that we are living in chaotic times. The infrastructure of our society is falling apart. Grade scores in schools are descending, and at the same time, the world is demanding more high-tech people who are knowledgeable in every area of life and science.

The times are as they were when King Asa and the citizens of the nation of Judah (the tribes of Judah and Benjamin) found themselves living in a chaotic condition. The Bible says the Spirit of the Lord came upon Azariah, the son of Oded, and he went to meet Asa, and said:

> ... Hear ye me Asa, and all Judah and Benjamin;
> The Lord is with you, while ye be with him; and if ye
> seek him, he will be found of you; but if ye forsake
> him, he will forsake you.
>
> 2 Chronicles 15:2

The next verse (v. 3) is the key to their situation: For a long period of time Judah had been without the true God, without a teaching priest, and without law.

> But when they in their trouble did turn unto the
> Lord God of Israel, and sought him, he was found of
> them.
>
> And in those times there was no peace to him
> that went out, nor to him that came in, but great
> vexations were upon all the inhabitants of the
> countries.
>
> 2 Chronicles 15:4,5

Chaos always has a cause — disobedience and rebellion against Almighty God. Asa and the children of Israel in Judah had forsaken God.

*Without God, there are no perimeters for living.

*Without God, there is no absolute right or wrong.

*Without God, everyone does what is right in his or her own sight. The rule of society today is "do your own thing."

The people of Judah had forsaken God and lived life without perimeters until Asa heard the words of the prophetic message from God. Then the king took courage. He put away the pagan altars. He renewed the altar of the Lord. He gathered all of Judah and Benjamin, and the strangers with them out of Ephraim and Manasseh, and out of Simeon.

People from the other tribes in the nation of Israel flocked to Jerusalem to worship with Asa "in abundance," when they saw that the Lord his God was with him. They made offerings to God and entered into a covenant with God. The terms of the covenant said that whosoever would not seek the Lord God of Israel should be put to death, whether they were rich or poor, man or woman.

> And they sware unto the Lord with a loud voice, and with shouting, and with trumpets, and with cornets.
>
> And all Judah rejoiced at the oath: for they had sworn with all their heart, and sought him with their whole desire; and he was found of them: and the Lord gave them rest round about.
>
> **2 Chronicles 15:14,15**

God brought them out of their chaotic condition, as He will bring us out individually or corporately (a local church or our nation) if we do as King Asa and the Judaites did.

Ten Steps Out of Chaos

There are ten truths in that story that are keys to help you get out of whatever chaotic condition that might exist in your life. Oftentimes people live very orderly lives with perhaps one area that is chaotic. As you read these truths, you need to apply them with a certain amount of wisdom. Jesus said that wisdom is justified of her children. (Matt. 11:19.) Asa heard words and applied them with wisdom.

The ten truths, five of which I will discuss in this chapter and five in the next, are:

1. Recognize chaotic conditions.

2. Resist chaotic conditions.

3. Reassess your priorities.

4. Responsibility — accept it.

5. React — proceed with purpose.

6. Reprogram your thinking.

7. Refuse chaotic company.

8. Renew your commitment to God.

9. Rest in the order of the Lord.

10. Recognize that the world is a chaotic place.

Recognize Chaotic Conditions

If you want to come out of chaotic conditions, or there is an area in your life that is chaotic, learn to recognize it. The Bible tells us in Proverbs 16:25:

> **There is a way that seemeth right unto a man, but the end thereof are the ways of death.**

In 2 Chronicles 15, the story of Asa and Judah, we see some signs of a chaotic condition. There was no peace. There were vexations. There was destruction, and there were adversities.

If there are areas of your life where there is no peace, areas where there is great vexation, destruction, and adversity, these are areas where chaos rules. You cannot deal with a chaotic area until you first recognize that things are not the way they are supposed to be.

For example, if you have lived in poverty all of your life, you probably think it is the norm to be poor, but it is *not* the norm to be poor. God did not create you to be poor. God created you to be prosperous. But you can get so used to living in poverty that in your mind it is the way people are supposed to live.

For example, counselors say women caught in abusive marital relationships stay in them because they think that is the way marriage ought to be. Probably that is the way their parents' relationships were. But that is not the way marriage is supposed to be. Abuse is a sign of a chaotic relationship.

You cannot come out of chaos until you first recognize the chaotic conditions. If the "way that seems right" is not working, do something else. I talk to people all of the time who are frustrated in life, and all they really need is to do something differently.

An old saying in the South says: "If you want to keep on getting what you're getting, just keep on doing what you're doing."

So, if something in your life is not working, do something differently. Recognize chaotic conditions and change the way you are doing things in that area.

Resist Chaotic Conditions

Asa took courage and resisted the chaos that was running in the life of his nation. Proverbs 16:9 says, **A man's heart deviseth his way: but the Lord directeth his steps**. Asa made a commitment to let the Lord direct his steps and to come out of chaos.

When you make a real commitment to come out of the chaotic conditions of your life, God will begin to direct your steps because He does not want you living in chaos. He wants you to have an orderly life.

Jesus said in John 10:10:

> **The thief cometh not, but for to steal, and to kill, and to destroy: I am come that they might have life, and that they might have it more abundantly.**

You see, God knows what you need to know and that is that abundant life does not just happen. There are some in the Body of Christ who are waiting for the man or woman of God to wave a hand over them and instantly change them from a chaotic condition into an orderly condition. It does not work that way. Abundant life does not just happen spontaneously or accidentally.

Abundant life happens when you make a commitment to living an abundant life. And, you cannot make a commitment to live an abundant life as long as you allow chaos to rule and reign in your life. You have to make a commitment to get out of chaos. You resist it, and then God directs your steps.

That is when Psalm 37:23 becomes a reality:

> The steps of a good man are ordered by the Lord:
> and he delighteth in his way.

In May 1994, I completed my 25th year in the ministry. My wife, Connie, and I have had a good time preaching over the last quarter of a century. If we were able to sit down today, one on one, with each reader, or to write a book that long, we could tell you of time after time when God put us in the right place at the right time. Most of the time, we did not even know He was orchestrating our steps.

When there is a commitment to get out of chaos, when you come to a place that you are willing to resist, when you say that this is not the way life is supposed to be, then God begins to direct your steps. God never leads your steps into something worse, but always into something better.

However, there will be times, as God is leading your steps into something better, when it looks as if you are going through something worse. But, if you trust God and see it through, you will find it was just a part of the process of God leading you to where He wants you to be.

Reassess Your Priorities

Asa and Judah lived in a time when people had pulled down the law and chosen abominable idols. When things got chaotic enough, they reassessed their commitment to God. They reassessed the way they were worshipping. They reassessed their lives.

Decide what is important in life and understand what God said in Jeremiah 29:13, "You will find Me when you seek Me with your whole heart."

The first thing to do in reassessing your life is to put away your "idols." An idol is anything that comes between you and God. Some Christians worship every evening at the "one-eyed idol." Instead of raising their hands and worshipping God, they click their fingers and worship all of the networks.

By the way, I am not preaching against television in itself. I have three television sets in my house. One of them actually has a remote that works. I am not preaching against cable. But I have learned how not to worship TV programs. Experts claim the average American watches six hours of television a day. Six hours! I cannot believe there *are* six hours of worthwhile programming a day.

An idol is anything that comes between you and God. If you do not have time to pray, you need to pull down your idols. Some people even make their families into idols, or their jobs or careers. A young man in the Bible had this problem. (Matt. 8:21,22.)

When he came to Jesus, the Lord said, "Follow Me."

The man said, "Let me go bury my father first."

Jesus said, "No, let the dead bury the dead. You follow Me."

That would not be acceptable in some family-value circles today.

I talked to a lady once, who said that she felt God wanted her in our church, although she was not attending. I asked her why she did not come and be a part of church then.

She said, "Well, my four-year-old boy doesn't like your junior church."

And I thought to myself, get a life! If her four-year-old boy is running her life now, what does she think he is going to do when he is fourteen years old?

If you do not come to church because Sunday is the only time your family has to be together, then your family should be together in church learning how to worship God. You need to reassess the priorities in your life and decide what is important. If you are reassessing with the right motives and values, you are going to put God first.

Jesus said:

> **Seek ye first the kingdom of God, and his righteousness; and all of these things shall be added unto you.**
>
> **Matthew 6:33**

And having established that first priority — seeking God and His Kingdom — then you establish other priorities. You prioritize your life.

Family is important in life.

Work is important in life.

Entertainment — sports, movies, or even sitting in front of your television — is an important part of your life.

But you must prioritize those activities. They are only wrong when you allow one of those lesser priorities to come between you and God.

I love to play golf, but you will not find me golfing on Sunday morning. You might find me golfing on Sunday evening, because we do not have church on Sunday evening. However, if I am called to preach somewhere else on Sunday evening, I do not play golf. I have my priorities right. Reassess your life.

Responsibility — Accept It

Do not blame everything on everybody else. I want to go on record that, in spite of my upbringing, I am not a victim! I was born and brought up in a poor family. I was told that I would never excel at anything in the world. I was lousy in sports and not very well-motivated, but I refused to be victimized or categorized by society. I chose to accept responsibility for myself.

Proverbs 24:16 says, **A just man falleth seven times, and riseth up again. . . .** That proverb is true because a just man accepts responsibility. A just woman accepts responsibility. The ten most powerful words in the English language are: *If it is to be, it is up to me.* Do not buy into the, "Well, I-didn't-get-any-breaks syndrome." Whatever "breaks" I have had have been because I prayed them down and prayed them through. I have "worked the Word" and kept working the Word in the face of adversity.

Years ago, I told my wife that one of these days we would have a huge church and people would say it was an overnight success. Today, we have an "overnight success" because we prayed it down, prayed it through, worked the Word, and saw the Word work. The Word still works with those who work with the Word. If something is to be in my life, it is up to me.

Abraham Lincoln is one of the greatest success stories of our history. He failed at the Illinois legislature. He went bankrupt in the store that he opened, was rejected twice when he asked someone to marry him, was voted out of the House of Representatives, and lost a senatorial election. However, he went on from all that failure to become one of the greatest presidents the United States has ever seen.

Lincoln understood that he was responsible for himself, and if anything was to be in his life, it was up to him. He could have been discouraged at any point, coming from a very humble background. Instead, he chose to accept responsibility and press on. You must press on.

The well-known nineteenth-century preacher, Charles H. Spurgeon, said that he prayed as if everything depended on God, but worked as if everything depended on him. That principle of Spurgeon's is still a formula for success — if you will take the responsibility for your life.

React — Proceed With Purpose

Asa heard the prophetic word from Azariah, the son of Oded, and proceeded purposefully. He pulled down the false altars and began to gather like-minded people around him. When people saw God's hand was with Asa, they began to flock to him. He was proceeding with purpose. Do not procrastinate. Do not just react to the chaos in your life, *act*. Proceed with purpose.

Proverbs 26:13 tells us:

The slothful man saith, There is a lion in the way; a lion is in the streets.

Have you ever met someone who always says, "I'm going to get around to it one of these days; I'm going to do it tomorrow"?

There is only one problem with tomorrow. Tomorrow never gets here. A steak house in east Texas has a big sign out front that reads, "Free steak tomorrow." And in all of the years they have been in business, they have never given away a free steak.

If you go in on Wednesday, see the sign, "Free steak tomorrow," and go back on Thursday to get your free steak — they simply point to the sign which still says, "Free steak *tomorrow*." The point is that tomorrow never comes. Do not procrastinate if you want order in your life.

For example, how many of you are working on your first million? All of us are. That is unless you are one of the few who have already made your first million.

Some of you have thought, "I'd like to be really prosperous. I'd like to be blessed. I'd really like to make something in life."

All you have to do is start, and without knowing it, since you have not made your first million, you have already started. One of our church members was phased out of a job because of a reduction, and he began to attend law school. When he turned 41 years old, he became an attorney. Society needs more Christian attorneys. He proceeded with purpose.

Do not procrastinate. Set goals. What are your goals in life? If you do not have any goals in life, you will never get anywhere. Set goals. Proverbs 13:15 tells us that **Good understanding giveth favour....** In other words, you make your breaks by the goals that you set. Set goals.

Where do you want to be ten years from now? You may say, "Well, Jesus is coming back."

I know that. But, what if He does not come back in ten years, or even in our lifetimes? I am expecting Him to come back. I am hoping He comes back. I am anticipating His second return. But if He does not, what then? Where are you going to be in the year 2005? Society is moving into a brand new millennium. Where are you going to be? Many people say they do not know.

What if Jesus does not come back in the year 2000? Without order, without direction, you are going to be nowhere. You will be going around the same mountain, doing the same things. Set some goals, and then when you set your goals, write a plan.

Habakkuk 2:2 advises us to:

> . . . **Write the vision, and make it plain upon tables, that he may run that readeth it.**

You know, I can go to any place in the country, start a church, and see some success if I apply myself. I can share with other pastors why my wife and I have been successful in building churches. I can show pastors how to start churches.

The reason is that when I was seventeen years old, God gave me a plan. God gave me a vision on how to start a church. And I wrote that plan down. I have lost the piece of notebook paper that I wrote that plan down on, but when I wrote it down, it was indelibly etched in my mind. I have the plan. Anytime you have God's plan for your life and have the plan written down, you can accomplish that plan. Write a plan.

In the next chapter, we will look at the other five steps that can bring you out of chaos into order in your life.

4

Reprogramming and Renewing Your Mind

Reprogram Your Thinking

The sixth step to getting out of chaos is *to reprogram your mind.* It is not enough to set goals and write plans. You must "reprogram" your thinking. Your brain is the most sophisticated computer in existence. In fact, the composition of the brain is what all computers were originally based on.

Your *mind,* then, is made up of all of the "programs" that have been entered into the brain-computer by you and others around you. A lot of people today have had to learn how to use a computer, and not always by choice. I had to learn how to use a computer. One thing I discovered about computers is that if you put junk in, you get junk out.

Is there anyone else who talks to the computer? Do you say bad things to your computer? Most of the time it is not the computer's fault. Now there are those odd occasions when your hard drive crashes, or there is a power surge and you lose everything on your desktop, or your battery runs down and you lose everything on your screen.

Most of the time, however, when you are fussing at your computer, there is nothing wrong with the computer. It is what you have put into it. Similarly, there is nothing wrong with your thinking, except what you have put into it or what you have allowed other people to put into it.

God was with Asa, king of Judah. However, Asa had to reprogram his thinking. Suddenly he was the center of a great move of God. God was with him. All of the people who wanted to be a part of what God was doing and wanted to be with Asa had to "reprogram" their thinking.

Proverbs 23:7 says, **For as he thinketh in his heart, so is he....** You are whatever you perceive yourself to be. You can do whatever you perceive yourself doing.

My family watched the 1994 Winter Olympics. I can tell you with certainty that all those athletes who won saw themselves winning before they took to the ski slope or the ice. They saw themselves winning. In fact, Olympic conditioning does not involve just physical conditioning nor just learning techniques. The field of motivation has advanced to the point where Olympic hopefuls are taught to think with "an Olympic attitude."

Man did not invent this concept. God put it in His Word. **As a man thinketh in his heart, so is he.**

You will be poor as long as you think poor.

You will be oppressed as long as you think you are oppressed.

You will flounder in life as long as you see yourself floundering.

However, the moment you reprogram your thinking, then you will be whatever you think that you are.

Proverbs 16:3 says:

Commit thy works unto the Lord, and thy thoughts shall be established.

Make that kind of commitment to God and decide to reprogram your thinking according to the Word of God. Decide that you are going to start seeing yourself as God sees you. You are going to start confessing about yourself what God has confessed about you. Quit talking as if you are a lowly worm struggling through a world of sin.

You are going to become more than a conqueror, because that is what God said you are.

You are going to be an overcomer, living in victory because that is what God said you are.

You are going to be the head and not the tail, above and not beneath (Deut. 28:13), because that is what God said you are.

You are going to be blessed in the basket and blessed in the store because that is what God said you are.

You are the blessed of God; you have the prosperity of God; you are the righteousness of God; you have the peace of God.

When you begin to set yourself in agreement with God, you will find God-thoughts filling your mind. Your thoughts will be established, and as your thoughts are established, the works of your life will be established. Get your thoughts in line with God. Get your thoughts in line with God's Word.   Philippians 4:13 says:

I can do all things through Christ which strengtheneth me.

You can do all things through Christ Who strengthens you. *Reprogram your thinking.*

Refuse Chaotic Company

The people round about Judah "fell out" from their provinces because they wanted to *leave chaotic company*, the seventh step or key to getting out of chaos. They went to Asa, who was setting Judah in order. Asa's name means "God has helped." Proverbs 23:20,21 says:

> Be not among winebibbers; among riotous eaters of flesh:
>
> For the drunkard and the glutton shall come to poverty: and drowsiness shall clothe a man with rags.

Do you have friends whose main interest in life is to party, party, party?

I was listening to a national radio program the other night. The host was interviewing four local high school students: three basketball players and a cheerleader. This particular host was affiliated with a local university. He asked the students if they were going to attend his university, and the three basketball players said yes, but the cheerleader said no. She said that, instead, she was going to attend the rival university.

When the host asked her why, she said, "Because it's a better party school. They have more fun over there."

He asked, "You're going to college for an education or to party?"

And she said, "To party."

I hope with whatever brain cells she has left when she is finished, she gleans a little education for the money that her parents will be spending. That is a chaotic mentality. Refuse chaotic company. Do not be among winebiblers, among riotous eaters of flesh, people who want to party and play all the time.

There is nothing wrong with playing sometimes. There is nothing wrong with eating good food. But, the drunkard and the glutton shall come to poverty and be clothed with rags, Solomon said. Stay away from chaotic company. If you want to move from chaos into order, you need to associate with people whom God has helped. Find some orderly friends.

Have you ever noticed that, when people get a little disgruntled in church, they do not talk to people who have their lives in order? They talk to people who also are disgruntled.

The amazing thing is that once two or three disgruntled people get together, they believe the church is going to fail if they leave. I have been pastoring for twenty-five years, trust me on this one: When disgruntled people leave, usually no one notices they are gone, unless it is to notice that the church is more peaceable.

You see, there is no such thing as a perfect church. If you are looking for a perfect church, you are going to be looking for a long time and when you find it, it is not going to be perfect. The minute you walk through the door, it will not be perfect any longer. There are always things that you will not like.

Half the time when I walk off the platform at my church, I turn to the musicians and say the music was too loud. But that is my personal preference. Some of my church members think it is not loud enough, or too mediocre, too white, too black, too motivational, or not motivational enough.

If you are chaotic, you can always find other chaotic people who will agree with your chaos. If you want to come out of chaos, identify with people who are orderly. That is what Proverbs 27:17 tells us: **Iron**

sharpeneth iron; so a man sharpeneth the countenance of his friend. Find some iron to hang around with. Do not allow the iron of your life to be dulled against a piece of cardboard. Iron sharpens iron. *Refuse chaotic company.*

Renew Your Commitment to God

Asa and Judah made a strong *renewal of their commitment to God*, the eighth key at which we want to look. They offered up seven thousand offerings to God, and they made a commitment to God. They made a covenant with God. They said anyone who did not seek after God would be killed.

How is that for revival? Those who did not turn to God (today we would say "become Christian") were taken out and shot with arrows. The altars would be full today. There would be people down in the altars who have never been at the altar and never intended on being at the altar, if that were the criteria.

Are you glad you are living under grace? Asa and Judah had revival, because they renewed their commitment to God. By the way, *God* did not tell them to kill anyone who did not seek Him with all of his heart. The Judaites took that on themselves. They were so filled with zeal that they wanted to make a commitment to God.

Do you want to see God's salvation? Then order your conversation aright. Order your lifestyle aright. Seek after God. Renew your commitment to God. Renew the covenant understanding that salvation is a process, which begins with the act of accepting Jesus as your Savior. After that, you grow in the grace and knowledge that is in Jesus Christ.

Day by day, you are renewed.

Day by day, you are restored.

Day by day, you come into a closer relationship with God.

Some of you reading this book need to renew your commitment to God.

Rest in the Order of the Lord

In the story of Asa and Judah, the Bible tells us that, after they came back into His order, *the Lord gave rest* round about, the ninth step or key that we see in this story.

Jesus said in Matthew 11:28:

> **Come unto me, all ye that labour and are heavy laden, and I will give you rest.**

When a life is in the midst of chaos, there is no rest. The reason cocaine is such a dangerous drug is that it disrupts the neural patterns of the brain and creates a constant state of chaos, in which there is no rest. Someone using cocaine can stay up for days as long as he keeps snorting the drug. But when he crashes, he crashes with a number of bad side effects. He has a chemically-induced chaotic mind, and there is no rest for him.

If your life is surrounded by chaos, your spirit has no rest. Let me suggest that you need to create an island of order in a sea of chaos. You are not going to make the world perfect. This is an imperfect world. But, you can create an island of order in important areas of your life in the middle of the "sea of chaos."

Fellowship: The church should be an island of order in the sea of chaos. Hebrews 10:25 says:

> Not forsaking the assembling of ourselves
> together, as the manner of some is; but exhorting one
> another: and so much the more, as ye see the day
> approaching.

If you believe that Jesus is going to return in this generation, then what manner of man or woman ought you to be in the faithfulness to the house of God? We should encourage one another, exhort one another, and build one another up. Fellowshipping with the saints should be an island of order in the midst of chaos.

Family: Your home and family ought to be an island of order in the midst of chaos, not a place of constant confusion, bickering, bitterness, and strife.

Friendships: Your friendships ought to be islands of order in the midst of chaos. You need to have the kind of friends whom you know are friends regardless of what happens, not the kind of friends to whom you have to continually and constantly prove yourself.

Finances: Certainly your finances ought to be islands of order in the midst of today's financial chaos! Ever so often I will pick up a magazine or newspaper with articles about difficult financial times that are ahead. I have several friends who believe the economy is going to crash in the next several years. It may, but if so, my finances will remain an island of order in the midst of chaos.

When the stock market crashed in 1929, there were as many people who became millionaires as there were who lost their millions. Those who became millionaires had their finances already in order. In fact, the reason the stock market crashed in 1929 was because of chaos. Keep your finances an island of order in the midst of chaos, and your future, if you are a child of God, will be taken care of.

Jesus said in Matthew 6:34:

Take therefore no thought for the morrow: for the morrow shall take thought for the things of itself.

*The Future: Your future ought to be an island of order in the midst of chaos. God has it under control. I may not know what is going to take place tomorrow, but I know the One Who does. I know whom I believe, and I am persuaded that He is able to keep that which I have committed to Him against that day. There can be order in the midst of chaos.

The tenth and final lesson we can learn about getting out of chaos from Asa and Judah is to remember that, simply because you have changed and come into order, that does not mean the world around you has.

Recognize That the World Is a Chaotic Place

The Bible says the "high places" (places on top of hills where heathen gods were worshipped) were not taken away out of Judah; nevertheless the heart of Asa was "perfect" all of his days. He came out of chaos into order.

You also will come out of chaos into order if you follow these ten truths. The story of Asa is a road map that we can follow from chaos into order.

However, your order can become chaotic. Your order can "create chaos," or be transformed again into chaos, if it becomes rigid and legalistic. At that point, you are not operating in God's order, but in tradition and religion. Jesus said new wine should be put in new wineskins. (Matt. 9:17.) That is because new wineskins have flexibility. Some readers may take this message and misapply it creating more chaos than order.

I have seen this happen. There was a man known for his orderliness, but whose family was out of order. He went to a men's retreat and learned about setting godly order in the home.

He told a friend, "I'm going to go home, take what I've learned, and establish godly order. From this time on, our house will be a house of order. I'm going to establish the fact that God has ordained that I be high priest of my household."

Well, he went home with the great teaching he had received in that men's retreat, walked in the door, and said, "Woman, I'm here to set this house in order."

A few weeks later he saw his friend, who asked, "How did things go when you went to set order in your home?"

"Well," he said, "I walked in the door, and I told my wife, 'Woman, I'm here to set order.'"

His friend said, "What happened?"

He said, "I didn't see her for two weeks."

"You mean she moved out?"

"No, it took that long for the swelling to go out of my eyes."

I have known parents who hear this message and go to their teenagers to "establish order." Perhaps they will say, "Your bedtime is now 8:30 p.m."And, when the teenagers ask why, the parents say, "Because Pastor said so."

But I did not say anything about an 8:30 p.m. bedtime for teenagers! Those parents go by the "letter of the law" and miss the spirit, or the principles, behind the "rules." (2 Cor. 3:6.)

You see, the world is a chaotic place. You are never going to have perfect order in this world, but you can have islands of order. In trying to perfect order, however, you must be careful not to create more chaos.

In the next chapter, I am going to discuss order in the house. There will never be order in your house until there is order in the house of God.

If you are reading this book, and you are not a Christian, you may want to be.

If you know your life is bound with chaos, and you want God to set you free from it, the first step is to know Jesus as your Savior. Pray these words:

> *Father God, forgive me of my sins, my trespasses, my shortcomings. Renew in me a clean heart. Restore my soul, change my mind, order my steps for righteousness sake. I thank You for Jesus dying on the cross and being resurrected on the third day. I confess with my mouth what I believe in my heart, and that is that Jesus Christ is the Son of God and Lord of all. (Rom. 10:9,10.) Most of all, He is Lord over my life. Order my steps. Order my life for good, in Jesus name. Amen.*

5

Order in the House of God

There has to be order in the church. I am not talking just about the kind of order that a staff of ushers provides, but the kind of atmosphere that comes when you understand spiritual order. It makes a difference when the congregation understands the order of the church and submits to that order. However, *order* in the church does not mean stilted, rigid services.

Do you know church can be funny? Some of the funniest things I have ever seen happened in a church service. For example, the first revival I ever held was in a small town in Oklahoma, and a lady gave 25 cents in the offering and asked for 15 cents change.

There was the time in our church in Indianapolis when I was preaching one night and having a prayer line. People were getting excited and shouting a little bit. Then this woman started dancing, and she danced her way out of her slip. I glanced over at her, and I saw her black half-slip laying around her ankles. The mishap did not faze her. She stepped out of the slip, kicked it under the pew, and kept right on dancing.

Then there was also the Sunday morning in the church we pastored in Lima, Ohio. Our building was at the corner of Main and Kibey streets, which is a real interesting corner because any kind of person might wander into the church. One particular Sunday morning, a young, tall man stood up at the back of the church. Just as the service begun, he walked down the side, crossed the middle section aisle, stopped at the corner, reached down and put his hand on top of one of the men's heads, looked around, marched on down the center aisle, and up on the platform.

By this time, I had motioned for the ushers, and when he looked around, there were six, big guys running up to the platform. I will never forget the look on that man's face. He looked as if he were going to die.

Then there was the fellow who visited our present church, Liberty Christian Cathedral in Dayton, Ohio, one Sunday morning. As the service was underway, this fellow walked down the center aisle, shoulders thrown back, arms pumping like he owned the joint. He came and sat on the front row and repeated everything I said in a very loud, obnoxious, grating voice.

I looked at him and asked, "Would you mind quieting down?"

At the end of the service, he came up in the prayer line and asked for prayer.

I said, "What do you need prayer for?"

He said, "I have lust problems."

I said, "You talk too loud too, but Jesus loves you anyway."

I have seen some strange things in church, but if you cannot have fun in church, where can you have fun?

Seriously, I really appreciated those ushers in Lima. If anyone came in to cause a disturbance, the ushers were always ready. They could handle any situation with great aplomb. They never made a scene and never caused anyone embarrassment, but they did know how to hustle someone to a side room if that person was disrupting the service.

And I appreciate the ushers at Liberty Christian Cathedral. They are great men dedicated to serving the congregation and helping to maintain order. You might not think ushering is any big deal, but can you imagine having a crowd of people without any kind of order at all?

Order Enhances Worship

Following are a few scriptures that tell of how we should feel when we come together to worship the Lord. People cannot be in the frame of mind talked about in these verses when the church services or the church itself operates chaotically. Look at Psalm 122:1-9:

> I was glad when they said unto me, Let us go into the house of the Lord.
>
> Our feet shall stand within thy gates, O Jerusalem. Jerusalem is builded as a city that is compact together:
>
> Whither the tribes go up, the tribes of the Lord, unto the testimony of Israel, to give thanks unto the name of the Lord.
>
> For there are set thrones of judgment, the thrones of the house of David.
>
> Pray for the peace of Jerusalem: they shall prosper that love thee.
>
> Peace be within thy walls, and prosperity within thy palaces.
>
> For my brethren and companions' sakes, I will now say, Peace be within thee.
>
> Because of the house of the Lord our God I will seek thy good.

Are you glad when they say, "Let us go into the house of the Lord?"

I certainly am. I look forward to Sunday morning. I look forward to getting up and going through the Sunday morning routine of getting the paper, having a leisurely cup of coffee, and checking out the television program from the church. By 9:15 a.m., we are on the road; and, by 9:35 a.m., we are at "the house of the Lord."

If you do not understand the house of God, you can be sad in church. In the first chapter, we looked at the story of the first offering under the law, where Abihu and Nadab offered up "strange fire" (the wrong incense) before the Lord, and God smote them. Do you realize there is a parallel in the New Testament? It is found in Acts 5:1-11.

Jesus' disciples were in the midst of a great revival. God was moving in a marvelous way. Miracles were taking place. The Church, the entire Body of Christ at that time, went from a hundred and twenty to three thousand, and then another five thousand people were added. The Church continued steadfastly in the apostles' doctrine and fellowship, Luke wrote.

Then chaos entered in. A certain man named Ananias and his wife, Sapphria, sold some land and apparently wanted to look "righteous," so they lied about how much of the money they were giving to the Church. The situation was that these first followers of Jesus had decided to sell houses and lands and bring the money to the disciples to distribute to everyone according to his or her needs.

This was not the disciples' idea, and no one made the people do this. *They had a choice.* Peter knew from the Holy Spirit this couple was lying when they came separately to the meeting place, each claiming they were giving the entire price which they received for the land.

God did not require them to sell the land and lay the money from the sale at the apostles' feet. No, that was something this couple voluntarily entered into. And after the land was sold, it was their choice as to whether to give everything or whether to keep part of the money. The sin was in laying a portion of the money at the apostles' feet and claiming it was the full price of the land.

Ananias lied to the Holy Spirit, and he died immediately. He was not glad that day when they said, "Let us go to the house of the Lord!" Great fear seized all who heard what happened to Ananias, as we can imagine.

Some young men came forth, wrapped his body, carried him out, and buried him. Three hours later his wife Sapphira walked into the meeting. Peter asked her if she sold the land for such and such? He gave her a chance to tell the truth and save herself, because she did not know what had happened to her husband.

But she lied as well, telling Peter, "Oh, yes, that's what we sold it for."

> Then Peter said unto her, How is it that ye have agreed together to tempt the Spirit of the Lord? behold, the feet of them which have buried thy husband are at the door, and shall carry thee out.
>
> And she fell down straightway at his feet, and yielded up the ghost: and the young men came in, and found her dead, and, carrying her forth, buried her by her husband.
>
> And great fear came upon all the church, and upon as many as heard these things.

Acts 5:9-11

That kind of immediate consequence for sin would bring some order in our churches and fellowships today, would it not? That makes you glad for God's grace, doesn't it?

What Was God Doing in the Jerusalem Church?

I have an idea that a few people started thinking twice about joining the apostles, because they saw that the consequences of lying to the Holy Spirit was death. We must assume from the context that Ananias and Sapphira died at the hand of God, just as Abihu and Nadab had. Then why is the same immediate retribution not occurring today?

Do you think God was a little tough on that couple?

Have you ever lied to God by telling Him you would do something, then not doing it?

Have you ever told Him that you would quit doing a certain thing, then you did not quit it?

If so, you have done exactly the same thing that Ananias and Sapphira did. Why did God not kill you?

Why did Ananias and Sapphira die as soon as they sinned? They died for the same reason the two sons of Aaron died instantly: God was implementing and establishing order in His people. The Israelites were to be examples of an orderly people of God in Old Testament times. The New Testament Church was to be, and was, an orderly people — for some years, at any rate.

The examples of immediate judgment were to show the rest of God's people that the wages of sin is death. Chaos kills. Whether it is instantly or after a period of time, if you are living in chaos, you are going to die before your time, even in the midst of order. Notice that it was not sinners who were called instantly to account, but God's people.

I know there are Christians who have died early because of sin, which is chaotic living, but they have not died as did Ananias and Sapphira. The reason death does not immediately reward sin for us is that God is not beginning a new part of His plan to redeem mankind through us, so because of Jesus, He has mercy on us.

Paul said specifically that all of the things told in Scripture were to be *ensamples* (examples) for us. He made examples of those who sinned in the beginning of Israel and those who sinned in the beginning of the Church.

In I Timothy 3:15, Paul wrote to Timothy:

> **But if I tarry long, that thou mayest know how that oughtest to behave thyself in the house of God, which is the church of the living God, the pillar and ground of the truth.**

Paul wrote to his "son in the faith" (v. 2) that if he was not able to visit him right away, these were the things Timothy ought to know to do in order to behave properly in the church.

In other words, Paul was saying, "These are the guidelines of order in the church, and you are to follow after these guidelines, Timothy, and walk in godly order."

Order Makes for a Happy Church

Do you know what happens when believers walk out of order? They die. They may not die physically, but they die spiritually; they die emotionally; they die financially; they die in a myriad of ways, because chaos always kills.

If you leave a church angry, that is chaos, and you will carry that same anger into the next church — assuming you find another church.

If you leave a church with unresolved problems, you carry the same problems into the next setting until those problems are resolved, because chaos kills.

There was a church which split in the last city where Connie and I pastored, and overnight, we gained one hundred people in our congregation. I would like to be able to say that our new additions were happy people, but they were not. They were sad people. They were mad people.

If they would have repented of their anger and allowed the Spirit of the Lord to minister to them, they could have been established in our church and blessed. But instead they carried that anger with them. They carried that hurt. And one by one we saw them fall away. One by one we saw them drop away until out of that original group only about three actually stayed with us. And those were the three people who had dealt with the hurts in their hearts. They were the ones who set themselves in order.

If you are going to be a part of the church, you have to understand that the church is an orderly place. Is there to be order in the house of God? Absolutely.

When there is order in a local church or in the Church at large, we *can* say with David, "I was glad when they said unto me, let us go into the house of the Lord."

We sing that psalm as a chorus in our church, and we sing it as written, *unto* the house of the Lord. However, God does not want us *unto* His house. God wants us *into* His house.

Jesus said in Matthew 23:13:

> But woe unto you, scribes and Pharisees, hypocrites! for ye shut up the kingdom of heaven against men: for ye neither go in yourselves, neither suffer ye them that are entering to go in.

God does not want us *unto*. He wants us completely in His house.

There are folks who come to church just to see what is going on.

There are folks who come to church to hear what is going to be preached that Sunday, perhaps to hear one specific message.

There are folks who come to church to see their friends, believe it or not.

Those may all be valid secondary reasons for going to church, but they are not the primary reason you should be going to church. You should be attending church because you are in the church. You are part of the Body of Christ assigned by God to attend a particular local fellowship.

Ask yourself whether you are in the church. Unto or into? If you are just unto the church, you are going to be standing in the door keeping other people out. But if you are into the church and a part of the church, you are going to be a part of an open door that brings others into the house of God.

Psalm 122:2 says, **Our feet shall stand within thy gates, O Jerusalem**. In the Bible, when *Jerusalem* is not used literally of the city, it is used as a spiritual type of the church. Hebrews 12:22,23 says:

> But ye are come unto mount Sion, and unto the city of the living God, the heavenly Jerusalem, and to an innumerable company of angels.
>
> To the general assembly and church of the firstborn, which are written in heaven, and to God the Judge of all, and to the spirits of just men made perfect.

You — the Christians of all ages — have come to this heavenly Jerusalem, according to the writer of Hebrews. Look at what else the Bible says about our feet standing in the gates of Jerusalem. Second Samuel 22:37 says, **Thou hast enlarged my steps under me; so that my feet did not slip.**

Our feet stand in "Jerusalem." If you want to stand for God, stand in the church.

Tithes and Offerings: Part of Order

When I became a Christian, I only knew two things about serving God because I did not come out of a traditional religious family. I am not a second-generation Pentecostal preacher. I knew nothing about the Bible.

However, I did know two things, and I have no idea where I picked this information up, but it is good information. You go to church on Sunday morning, and you pay your tithes. Those are the only two things I knew about serving God when I became a Christian.

I did not know about the baptism of the Holy Ghost.

I did not know about the gifts of the Spirit.

I did not know about divine healing.

I did not know that God could prosper and bless me.

But I did know that, if I was a Christian, I was supposed to be in church on Sunday morning, and when I got to church, I was supposed to pay my tithes.

The first Sunday after I was saved, I paid 75 cents tithe and gave a 25-cent offering out of the $7.50 I had made. I was only fifteen years old. The next week, I mowed lawns and made $15. I went to church the next Sunday, because I was a Christian, and Christians go to church. Remember? Our feet stand in Jerusalem.

Let me interject here that it is not the one who starts the race who wins; it is the one who finishes it. There are many people who get off to a good start, but do not finish the course. There are others who do not get off to quite as fast a start, but they have staying power. They are always there.

At any rate, on the second Sunday, I paid my $1.50 tithe and made a 50-cent offering. I did not even need to write my name on the envelope, but I did. They could always tell my envelope because I drew smiley faces and doodled all over it. Sometimes, I put little happy sayings all over it, because before I became a Christian, I was miserable. After I became a Christian I was filled with joy because God had begun to bless me.

I did not understand anything about blessing or prosperity or the blessing of the house resting on my house, but I had sowed my 75-cent tithe and my 25-cent offering. The next week, I made double the amount of the previous week and doubled my tithe and offering. I knew something was working, but I did not understand what was working.

A week after that, I got a "real" job making $1.25 an hour, working forty hours a week in the hot, Texas sun. At the end of the week, I was paid with a little, brown manila envelope filled with $5 and $1 bills. I had $60. I thought I was rich.

As soon as I got home with that little envelope of money, I went into my bedroom and counted it all out. Then I counted it out again. After I counted it out the second time, I set aside the $6 tithe. I thought about it for a little bit, and I set aside a $4 offering. Then, I took that $10 and stuck it under my mattress because I did not want to take a chance on spending it before Sunday morning.

I had $50 left, so I jumped into my pickup truck and headed to a local discount store for the "blue-light" special, hitting every special they had that night. As a Christian I knew I had to set aside my tithe and my offerings, and God did not mind what I did with the remaining $50, as long as it was not used sinfully.

Order Brings Stability

When your feet stand within the gates of Jerusalem, God enlarges your steps so that you will not fall. Standing implies stability. First Corinthians 15:58 says:

> **Therefore, my beloved brethren, be ye stedfast, unmoveable, always abounding in the work of the Lord, forasmuch as ye know that your labour is not in vain in the Lord.**

The world is looking for stability. God is looking for stability. And the whole purpose of this book, *Order Out of Chaos*, is to bring people into a place of stability. God never intended for the Christian walk to be an up-and-down roller-coaster ride with things going good one day and bad the next, moving from one crisis to another crisis.

God does not move supernaturally to bail you out of a crisis for you to find yourself back in another one. The opposite of 1 Corinthians 15:58 is found in Ephesians 4:14:

> **That we henceforth be no more children, tossed to and fro, and carried about with every wind of doctrine, by the sleight of men, and cunning craftiness, whereby they lie in wait to deceive.**

You do not need the latest revelation in order to have a real relationship with God. I wrote earlier that what killed the charismatic movement was three words: Revelation without order. Everyone had to get the latest teaching. And there is only so much good teaching. There is only so much revelation, deep revelation. Most people who have what they call "deep revelation" are nuts.

God is calling us to a place of stability. We stand within the gates of Jerusalem. There is stability in the gates of Jerusalem and there is strength in the gates of Jerusalem because the gate implies strength. Jesus said in Matthew 16:18:

> **. . . And upon this rock I will build my church; and the gates of hell shall not prevail against it.**

Jesus is building a church that is a strong church. If you are a part of that Church, you are a strong believer. You are a stable believer. You are a standing believer. You are not going to be moved. You are not going to be shaken. Whatever comes, whatever goes, you are going to be there right in the midst of it seeing God move and manifest His power and presence in your life.

Ephesians 2:20 tells us the Church is built on the foundations of the apostles and prophets with Jesus Christ being the chief cornerstone. Paul wrote:

> In whom all the building fitly framed together
> groweth unto an holy temple in the Lord:
>
> In whom ye also are builded together for an
> habitation of God through the Spirit.
>
> Ephesians 2:21,22

The foundation of the Church is the ministry of the apostles and prophets. Jesus, the Chief Cornerstone, points that foundation in the right direction and causes it to be stable. When the Church is built on the foundation of the apostles and prophets, you have strength and stability, and God's people stand.

Acts 2:42 says that the first Christians continued steadfastly in the apostles' doctrine and fellowship. The Church added believers from the first one hundred and twenty to eight thousand, and then in Acts 6, we are told that the Church began to multiply! And the first-century Church was built.

A church, a real church, is not just a group of people getting together on Sunday morning. A real church becomes a habitation of God through the Spirit. Jesus told us where He would be, if we allow the Spirit to "fitly join" us together:

> Where two or three are gathered together in my
> name, there am I in the midst of them.
>
> Matthew 18:20

We come together corporately as a Body of Christ. Jesus is in our midst, and because He is in our midst, you can expect Him to minister and meet the needs of your life. Jerusalem is built as a city that is "compacted" together. (Ps. 122:3.) The Apostle Paul directly tied this idea from the psalms to the Body of Christ.

> **From whom the whole body fitly joined together**
> **and compacted by that which every joint supplieth,**
> **according to the effectual working in the measure of**
> **every part, maketh increase of the body unto the**
> **edifying of itself in love.**
>
> **Ephesians 4:16**

The word *compact* in Psalm 122:3 does not simply mean that the building is merged or pressed together. The word *compact* is from the Hebrew word, *chabar*, and it means "to join (lit. or fig.), by means of spells," or "to charm" as well as "to fellowship together."[2]

Compacting Reinforces Stability

David was not just writing about setting a few programs into place to keep people tied together through activities. When he wrote about being "compacted together," David was talking about supernatural work done by the Spirit of God, knitting the people one to another. You need people.

In Ephesians 4:16, the Greek word for *compact* is *sumbibazo*, which means "to drive (or force) together," or "to knit together," among other similar meanings.[2] First Corinthians 12:13 tells us that by one Spirit — the Holy Spirit — we are baptized into one Body, whether we are male or female, rich or poor, or of any race. (Gal. 3:28.) And we are made to drink of that one Spirit.

First Corinthians 12:27 says that we, literally, by the operation of the Spirit of God, become the Body of Christ. We become members in particular who are "compacted together" into one unit. Ephesians 5:30 says that **we are members of his body, of his flesh, and of his bones**. The Church is forcibly knit together by the Spirit of God.

As soon as you become born again, you become part of the Body of Christ. You have no choice in whether you are a part of it or not. Your only choice is whether to accept Jesus as your Savior. Once you have done that, the Holy Spirit automatically "knits" you into the Body.

Some believers are the feet. Some are the hands. Some are the eyes. Some are the mouthpiece. Every believer has a place in the Body; every believer is *in* the Body. You need to find where you fit and then let the Spirit of God cause you to fulfill your purpose there.

You can be an integral part of the Body, as is every believer, and still be kicking and fighting against the other parts, causing chaos. Too many Christians today are doing just that and hindering, if not paralyzing, the Church.

What does it mean to you personally to be an integral part of the Body? It means you are important. It means you have a part to play in the plan of God. It means that you fit in the house of God. It means that as you supply whatever it is God has called you to supply in the Body, the Church is going to grow, corporately and locally. It is going to increase and edify itself in love.

For example, one gentleman at our church opens the building for services. Opening the building is his ministry. He does a good job of opening the building and a good job of closing the building. There may be someone who thinks that opening and closing a church building is not important. However, it has to be done. Someone has to open and close the building. That makes it important.

You have a ministry gift in you. There is something God has placed in you that the Church needs. And there is something God has placed in you that demands fulfillment. You will never be happy even as a Christian until you find the place where God wants you to fit in the Body and then are fulfilled in that place. The Church is compacted together. It is knit together supernaturally by the Spirit of God.

Another area of society that is in chaos is the relationships of races one to another. God's order in this area is quite different from man's, as we will see in the next chapter.

Endnotes

[1] *Strong's*, "Hebrew Dictionary," p. 36, #2266.
[2] *Ibid.*, "Greek Dictionary," p. 68, #4822.

6

Tribes, Testimonies, Thrones, and Preservation

The Bible tells us in several places that the tribes of Israel "went up" to give thanks unto the name of the Lord. And, because of the Day of Atonement and other festivals, we know they must have "gone up" hundreds of times to the Tabernacle or the Temple. David mentions this in Psalm 122:3,4:

> Jerusalem is builded as a city that is compact together:

> Whither the tribes go up, the tribes of the Lord, unto the testimony of Israel, to give thanks unto the name of the Lord.

There are four words concerning that second verse which speak to us of order and chaos, of eternal things, and of victorious living in God's order in the midst of a chaotic world. The words are *tribes, testimony, thrones,* and *preservation.*

We know what "tribes" were in the Old Testament, but what are "tribes" today? Ephesians 2:14,15 gives us a clue:

> For he is our peace, who hath made both one, and hath broken down the middle wall of partition between us;

> Having abolished in his flesh the enmity, even the law of commandments contained in ordinances;

for to make in himself of twain one new man, so making peace.

Enmity is the unreasonable dislike of another person, because of his or her race or status or position in life. In the mind of God, in His ordering of the earth after the fall of Adam and Eve, there are only two races on planet earth: *Those who are born again, and those who are not.* If everyone in the Church could understand this, it would eliminate a lot of chaos in the Body.

*Society looks at things in terms of earthly races and cultures.

*God looks at mankind in terms of "born again" or "not born again."

In the Old Testament, God's "race" was called Israel, and later, Jews. The rest of mankind were called *idolators*, because they worshipped other gods. Literally, the Hebrew word *goy* means "a foreign nation" or "heathen." In the New Testament, *Gentile* translates two Greek words: *ethnos*, which means "a non-Jewish tribe," by implication, "a pagan," and *hellas*, which means a "Greek-speaking person."[1]

If you know Jesus as your Savior, you are part of the family of God.

If you do not know Jesus as your Savior, you are not part of the family of God.

If you know Jesus, you are going to heaven; if you do not know Jesus, you are going to hell. It does not make any difference whether you are white or black, red or brown. Hell and heaven are "equal opportunity" places.

Jesus took the "twain," Jew or Israelite (those with God, or those of God) and Greek (Gentile, heathen, or those without God) and He made of the two *one* man in

Jesus. That "one man" — Jesus and His Body — is "the tribes of the Lord" under the New Covenant.

That "one man" is going where his Head goes, and that is to heaven. If you are not part of that Man, you will go to the other place. There are only two places in eternity, which operate according to God's order.

Racism Is Part of Chaos

I saw a program once on television about the lost tribes of Israel. The theme of the program was the question: "Where are the ten lost tribes of Israel?"

Personally, I have no idea where they are, and quite honestly, I do not care. I am not concerned about the ten lost tribes of Israel. I am not concerned about the whereabouts of the lost ark of the covenant. I concern myself with what I am called to do, with what is going to edify me, with what is going to build me up.

I am concerned with the fact that if any man be in Christ, he is a new creature. (2 Cor. 5:17.) Jews and Gentiles have become one new man. (Gal. 3:28; Eph. 2:15.)

Some people research their genealogy to find out about their ancestors and where they came from. One summer, I found out more than I really cared to know about my family history. My mother came to visit us, and she had been researching her genealogy. Why, I don't know.

However, she told me that one of my great-aunts had operated a bordello in the northern part of Georgia. That information is something I could have lived without!

I want to know my spiritual genealogy — **to make in himself of twain one new man, so making peace**

(Eph. 2:15). When you come to the understanding that there are only two races on planet earth in the sight of God, those born again and those who are not, you have peace.

Culturally, people are different. They have been since the Tower of Babel, when God "confused" the languages and scattered the people. (Gen. 11:1-9.) Their perversion of order — using one language to rebel against God rather than to come to God — resulted in chaos. Therefore, various cultures began to develop as the groups of people became isolated from one another.

Today, Northerners are different from Southerners, Easterners are different from Westerners. Europeans are different than Americans. Every portion of the globe has its own culture different in at least some ways from every other. There are regional and racial cultures.

Appreciate your culture, because it helped shape you. That culture is a part of your being, your makeup, but do not stake your eternal life on your culture. Stake your eternal life on the One Who paid the price to lift you out of the slavery of chaos. (1 Cor. 7:23.)

The permanent, eternal culture of the children of God is found in the heavenlies of which we are given glimpses in the Bible. Our genealogy is God and Abraham through Jesus Christ, our elder Brother, Savior, Lord, and King. (Rom. 8:17; Gal. 3:7,29.) If you are a member of the other race, cultures, genealogies, earthly races, and languages will be totally no good to you in hell. (Rev. 20:12-15.)

The Word of Our Testimony

The second word we want to look at is *testimony*. Hebrews 10:25 says:

> Not forsaking the assembling of ourselves
> together, as the manner of some is; but exhorting one
> another: and so much the more, as ye see that day
> approaching.

"Whether the tribes go up, the tribes of the Lord to the testimony of Israel" is not just history relegated to the Old Testament Israelites. The principle applies to God's people of any era.

Do you know that when you get into your car each Sunday morning on your way to church, your neighbors get a testimony?

Do you know when you walk into your church doors, you are giving a testimony? You are saying that it is important to you to be in the house of God. The church is a place of testimony where your witness shines out. And the church is a place of thanks. Psalm 100:4 says:

> Enter into his gates with thanksgiving, and into
> his courts with praise: be thankful unto him, and bless
> his name.

Have you ever noticed that you can come into church tired from a day's work or tired from a busy week, yet when the music and worship begin, something happens that is energizing? There is something invigorating in fellowshipping together before the Lord.

The Spirit of the Lord begins to move in your spirit. Suddenly, your tiredness is all gone. You begin to think of the good things God has done in your life. You begin to respond in thanksgiving and in praise. Church is a place of thanksgiving where we give thanks unto the name of our God.

The Tribes of the Lord, that is, those of us born by the Spirit of God, "go up" to bring testimony to Him.

The church manifests in our lives as a place of thanksgiving.

A Place Where Thrones Are Set

The third word to consider in that verse is *thrones.* The church is a place where thrones are set. *Thrones* in the Bible are places of judgment, as well as places of reigning. David continued to explain what happened when the "tribes went up" unto the "testimony of Israel" in Psalm 122:5:

> For there are set thrones of judgment, the thrones of the house of David.

First Peter 4:17 carries this thought into the Church:

> For the time is come that judgment must begin at the house of God: and if it first begin at us, what shall the end be of them that obey not the gospel of God?

Judgment is a time when order must be brought out of chaos. I do not like having to be the instrument of judgment, yet sometimes it is necessary, both in the pulpit and at home. When our children were growing up, ever so often they would get rowdy. They would go as far as they could go, as all children do, and as I am sure you and I also did.

However, there would come a time when, as a responsible parent, I would have to say, "All right, children. If you get out of line, you're going to get swift, sure judgment this week, not mercy. And, because mother and I always keep our word, we will have judgment week."

By the end of that week, everyone was settled down, ready to live in order again. Usually, the children were in line for another six months. Of course, "judgment" was never abusive punishment, only quick correction. "Correction" means to put something or someone back on course. A child should be corrected, not punished.

We believe that if you train up children in the way they should go, when they are old they will not depart from the ways of God. (Prov. 22:6.) We instilled the concept of judgment in our children, that you reap what you sow (Gal. 6:7), unless you repent; then God's mercy wipes out the offense through the blood of Jesus.

The time has come when judgment must begin at the house of God. Ananias and Sapphira found out about judgment. And judgment in the Church today, just as in the days of the apostles, must first begin with individuals. Judgment affects each part of the Body; in other words, it begins with you and with me.

Paul asked, "What will be the end of them who do not obey the gospel of God?" (2 Thess. 1:8.)

The end is judgment, he said, referring to those who do not receive Jesus.

However, Christians also must come up for judgment, not for salvation but for works done, good or bad, that bring rewards. (Rev. 20:12,13.) There is one sure way for a Christian to avoid judgment. You can find that way in 1 Corinthians 11:31:

> **For if we would judge ourselves, we should not be judged.**

If you will judge yourself, you will be quick to repent and be forgiven. (1 John 1:9.) You will not come under God's judgment. But, if you do not judge yourself, you will come under judgment because the Church is the pillar and ground of the truth, which means the standard is set in us.

If each part of the Church does not judge itself according to that standard and set itself in order according to that standard, that part will come under judgment.

Again, let me make it clear that I am not talking about salvation or about going to heaven. I am talking about whether you live in God's order which brings victory in this life, or whether you live in the disorder of chaos because of disobedience or rebellion in a certain area. If you persist in doing your own thing and going your own way, then you will find yourself:

*Under judgment

*Out from underneath the covering of the Church and the Holy Spirit Who give you spiritual protection

*Open to the attacks of the enemy

*Without any spiritual authority

Authority Brings Authority

There is a second concept involved in judgment, one which I mentioned in the last chapter. You need to understand clearly that *order has its own inherent power.* In Matthew 8:9, the Roman centurion seeking healing for his servant told Jesus that he understood authority.

> **I am a man under authority, having soldiers under me: and I say to this man, Go, and he goeth; and to another, Come, and he cometh; and to my servant, Do this, and he doeth it.**

In other words, he was saying, "I'm under authority, and I have authority. I understand how authority works. And I can see that You have spiritual authority over sickness, disease, and demons. I know that if You will just speak, things will get done."

If you are not under authority, you do not have authority. You may invoke the name of Jesus, you may pray all the right prayers, you may say all the right things, but if you are not under authority, you do not have authority. Such a simple concept — yet we ignore it, rebel against it, and get ourselves into chaos. Set yourself in order, according to the guidance of the Word of God and the Holy Spirit, and no one else will have to set you in order.

Hebrews 13:17 talks about submitting yourself to those who are in authority over you, the same issue dealt with in 1 Peter 2:13. When we set ourselves under authority, we have authority, and the blessing of the house rests upon our house.

The rest of Psalm 122, verses 6-9, says:

> **Pray for the peace of Jerusalem: they shall prosper that love thee.**
>
> **Peace be within thy walls, and prosperity within thy palaces.**
>
> **For my brethren and companions' sakes, I will now say, Peace be within thee.**
>
> **Because of the house of the Lord our God I will seek thy good.**

First, David gives a prayer priority. Pray for the peace of Jerusalem, or pray for the peace of the Church.

If you hear someone talking badly about your church, set them straight. Any church has at least two disgruntled people in it. Those two will always find one another, and they will talk. And because they are disgruntled, they will try to find someone else who is happy to get into their "disgruntledness," which is why David said, pray for the peace of the Church.

At one point in David's life, the Kingdom was fairly settled, and David had built a palace in Jerusalem for himself and his household. The Bible says that he began to think about his good situation and to feel badly that the ark of the covenant was still in a tent (the tabernacle) with no permanent building for God.

As it turned out, God did not want David to build the temple, because he had all of the shed blood on his hands that had been involved in dealing with Israel's enemies. (2 Sam. 7:1-16.) David's son, Solomon, built the temple. (1 Kings 4-6), but it was David who really had a heart for the house of God.

Get a heart for the house. Make the church your priority in prayer. Pray that God will bless the church, that God will bless the ministry. If you want a good pastor, pray for your pastor all the time. Pray for the peace of the house, because in it there is prosperity, and prosperity is what you are getting out of it. The blessing of the house will rest on your house. As God prospers the church, God prospers you.

When I first started pastoring, God spoke to me and said, "Preach two scriptures to the people":

> . . . Believe in the Lord your God, so shall ye be established; believe his prophets, so shall ye prosper.
>
> **2 Chronicles 20:20**

> Bring ye all the tithes into the storehouse, that there may be meat in mine house, and prove me now herewith, saith the Lord of hosts, if I will not open you the windows of heaven, and pour you out a blessing that there shall not be room enough to receive it.
>
> **Malachi 3:10**

Connie and I built our first church on those two concepts. The first year I preached, I preached them every service to build a base of blessing in the church.

People would come into the church poor and upset, and falling apart. God would put them back together, and they would start to prosper. There is a blessing on the house. There is prosperity in that blessing.

If you love the house of God, then God said you are going to prosper. And that word *prosper* in the Hebrew means "to push forward in various senses," and in the Greek, "to succeed in business affairs."[2] You are going to have success. You will start a thing, and you will push forward to finish it. God will bless you in the doing of it.

God promises prosperity and peace to those in His house. Peace be within thy walls. When you are in the house, there is peace.

Solomon, the second son of David and Bathsheba, was chosen to succeed his father on the throne of Israel. (1 Kings 1.) *Solomon* means "peaceful."[3] When you settle yourself in the house of God, there is peace because you are not tossed this way and that way by every wind of doctrine.

There is peace because you have built strong, stable relationships that endure in difficult times.

There is peace because when you are troubled in your mind and troubled in your life, you can come to church, hear the word of God, and fellowship with the saints of God, and find peace in the house of God.

There Is Preservation

Finally, the fourth word which we are considering is *preservation*. First Chronicles 17:12 tells us of God's words concerning Solomon: **He shall build me an house, and I will stablish his throne for ever.** That is preservation!

There are many promises of preservation for the people of God, particularly in the psalms. (Ps. 91.) We have proved those scriptures true in our own lives.

When we pastored the church in Lima, we obtained an old theater building. We had no money to buy it. God just supernaturally put us in it. We spent everything we had remodeling and renovating that building. It had been built in 1918 and had glass all across the front.

During the last service in the little storefront building where we started, a policeman came in the back door and motioned for someone to come out and talk with him. Our church secretary listened to him, then slipped out the back door with a funny look on her face.

As I wound up my sermon, of course I was wondering what was going on. I just knew something had happened to the theater building. An hour later, the secretary came back. The service was over by that time, so I could ask her what was going on.

There had been an accident at our corner. Two cars had collided so hard that the fenders and tires were knocked completely off of one of them, which was thrown up against our theater building. I pictured in my mind old, brittle glass shattered everywhere. I expected the worst. We were supposed to move into it the next week.

But when I asked her what had happened to the building, she said, "Nothing"! She said there was one six-inch gash on a concrete pillar about a half-inch deep, and there was not any broken glass. It was a miracle.

You would not believe it if you saw it. One car was completely up against the front of our building, yet there was no damage. She said it had to be preservation. God preserves His house.

If you are in the house, God will preserve you. Is there order in the house? Find your place in the house and you will have preservation. You will have peace. You will have prosperity, and you will find your priorities in God.

Remember:

*Racism is part of chaos. No matter what race, gender, or class you are of, there are only two "tribes," or races in God's order: the saved and the unsaved.

*Your life is a testimony to order or to chaos.

*Thrones are set in the Church.

*Find your place in the house of God, and you will have preservation.

Endnotes

[1] *Strong's*, "Hebrew and Chaldee Dictionary," *goy*, p. 26, #1471; "Greek Dictionary," *ethnos*, p. 25, #1484, and *hellas*, p. 27, #1672.

[2] *Ibid.*, "Hebrew and Chaldee Dictionary," p. 99, #6743; "Greek Dictionary," p. 33, #2137.

[3] *Ibid.*, "Hebrew and Chaldee Dictionary," p. 117, #8010,

7
God-Ordered Steps

As we have seen in the earlier chapters, and as most of us already know, we are living in a chaotic world, a chaotic society, and a chaotic time.

It is good to know whom you believe.

It is good to know what you believe.

If I did not know the Lord, I would be miserable. But I read the end of the Book. I found out how this world of chaos ends up — and our side wins.

In Psalm 37:23, we read that the steps of a good man are ordered of the Lord, and He delights in that man's way. God desires to order your steps, and you certainly need God-ordered steps. If you are not walking in God-ordered steps, you are probably walking out of order and without direction.

Pioneer woodsman Daniel Boone once said, when he was blazing new trails through North Carolina, Tennessee, and Kentucky, "If you do not care where you are going, you are never lost."

Yet, if you do not know where you are, you *are* lost. Sometimes when I am in a strange city, I like to take long, aimless, rambling walks. I find them to be relaxing. Oftentimes, I see things that otherwise I would not see.

Even in my long, aimless, rambling walks, I want to get back to the point of my departure. It is one thing to take an ambling, rambling walk because you want to get out and see what you can see, but it is another thing to live that as a lifestyle.

You need, I need, we all need God-ordered steps. In the book of Genesis 5:24, the Bible says, **Enoch walked with God: and he was not; for God took him.** He had such a walk with God that he never tasted of death. One moment Enoch was walking along through life with God, and the next moment, God took him into the heavenlies.

In Genesis 17:1, we find that God called His covenant-partner Abraham in an ordered walk.

> **And when Abram was ninety years old and nine, the Lord appeared to Abram, and said unto him, I am the Almighty God; walk before me, and be thou perfect.**

God called Abraham to an ordered walk, just as God has called us to an ordered walk. We always come to a place in our Christian walk where we can yield ourselves to God and say, "Take over, take control," and God begins to order our steps. If we do not say that, we continue to live in chaos.

In 2 Kings 2, Elijah and his servant, Elisha, set out on Elijah's last journey. *Elijah* means "God of Jehovah" or in a manner of speaking, "God Himself."[1] *Elisha* is a shortened form of *Eliyahuwa*, which means "God of supplication (or of riches)."[2] The two men proceeded from Gilgal to Bethel to Jericho to the Jordan River, and at each place, Elijah said to Elisha, "You stay here."

And each time Elisha replied, **As the Lord liveth, and as thy soul liveth, I will not leave thee.** Elisha understood that if he followed Elijah, in the meaning of

Elijah's name, he would obtain God's salvation. And in 2 Kings 2:9-15, we see that Elisha inherited a double portion of the anointing that was on Elijah, because he allowed his steps to be ordered by God.

Do you want your steps ordered by God? Are you willing to trust God in ordering your steps? Before you answer, you need to know that God may order your steps in a direction that you do not want to go. God may say to go one way, and you want to go another way.

God's Ways Are Not Our Ways

God ordered the steps of one of Abraham's great-grandsons, Joseph, in a way that he would not have chosen for himself. However, he ended up at a very good place, and only the path God had chosen could have gotten him there.

Genesis 37:3 says that Israel (Jacob) loved Joseph more than all his children, because he was the son of his old age. The name Joseph means, "let him add."[3] In the eyes of his father, Joseph was the promise that there would be years added to Jacob's life, that his genealogy would be carried on. He saw in Joseph his heart's desires being fulfilled.

Jacob, renamed *Israel* by God (Gen. 32:28), made Joseph a coat of many colors, which represents the tapestry of life, the multiple-dimensioned facets of life.

You see, your life is not a pane of glass letting light through. Your life is a diamond that refracts and reflects the light out. The light of Jesus shines into your life, and then you are to reflect that Light out to others. Your life is a coat of many colors.

I walked through a shoe store some time ago, and I happened to have our youngest daughter, Becka, with me. She has heard the story of my younger days when I used to wear a lot of bright colors. In the shoe store, they had a pair of orange, crocodile shoes.

She said, "Dad, do you want those?"

I looked at her, and said, "Babe, there *was* a day — but not now."

Historically, bright colors have reflected life. Joseph had a coat of many colors. The coat of many colors was a covering. It kept him from the sun in the day and the cold at night. The Bible tells us in Romans 13:14 about our covering:

> **But put ye on the Lord Jesus Christ, and make not provision for the flesh, to fulfill the lusts thereof.**

In the tapestry of your life, you are covered with the blood of Christ. You have put on Christ. When God the Father sees you, He does not see you in your imperfections. He sees you in the perfection that is Christ. The coat was a covering.

Secondly, the coat was an expression of joy. It was "loud."

Do you remember Reverend Ike? Back in the seventies, he would tell his followers to wear their brightest colors because "if you're going to a party, you don't dress like you're going to a funeral." That is a true saying.

The coat of many colors represented an expression of life, a joy-filled quality life. Jesus wants you to have fun. Somewhere along the line, the Church has been brainwashed that, if you are a Christian, you will never enjoy yourself.

The religious idea of Christianity is that you are not supposed to laugh. You go to work. You go home. You watch Christian television. You go to bed. You get up the next morning. You go to work. You go home. Eat. Watch Christian television. Go to bed. You attend the midweek church service if you are not too tired. Church is supposed to be very quiet, solemn, and boring.

In Nehemiah 8:10, we read the truth about how the life of God's people should be:

> Then he said unto them, Go your way, eat the fat, and drink the sweet, and send portions unto them for whom nothing is prepared: for this day is holy unto our Lord: neither be ye sorry; for the joy of the Lord is your strength.

The multi-colored coat of Joseph is symbolic of the joy that you and I ought to experience as believers. Isaiah said that we draw waters out of the well of salvation with our joy. (Isa. 12:3.) You want to be a happy Christian? Let the joy of the Lord loose in your life, and you will find that the joy of the Lord will be your strength.

The coat of many colors was a thing of opulence. It was expensive. Do you like fine clothes? When I started preaching, the only clothes I could afford were the ones I bought at the Goodwill Store and thrift shops. I remember buying a sport coat one day for $1.25 and feeling badly at spending that much money on a sport coat!

I weighed a hundred and twenty pounds in those days, but I would always buy a size 42 coat. I could have wrapped the coat around myself and used it for a blanket. I had two pairs of cheap slacks and one pair of beatup shoes. God has brought us a long way since then.

That coat of many colors was expensive. It was fine material. And it speaks of our riches as believers.

It speaks of our redemptive riches. First, the spiritual has to precede the natural, but the church gets messed up. It gets things backwards. As Christians, we want the natural to precede the spiritual, redemptive riches.

Ephesians 1:18-23 says:

> The eyes of your understanding being enlightened; that ye may know what is the hope of his calling, and what the riches of the glory of his inheritance in the saints,
>
> And what is the exceeding greatness of his power to us-ward who believe, according to the working of his mighty power,
>
> Which he wrought in Christ, when he raised him from the dead, and set him at his own right hand in the heavenly places,
>
> Far above all principality, and power, and might, and dominion, and every name that is named, not only in this world, but also that which is to come:
>
> And hath put all things under his feet, and gave him to be the head over all things to the church,
>
> Which is his body, the fulness of him that filleth all in all.

What does all of that mean? It means we are redeemed. Not only are you redeemed, you are seated in heavenly places in Christ Jesus. God has shown us the riches of the glory of His grace by revealing it in the person of Christ. "Put on" the Lord Jesus Christ, and make no provision for the flesh to fulfill its desires, Paul wrote.

The Christian Life Is Opulent and Rich

The coat was a thing of opulence and riches, just as God's redemptive plan is a thing of opulence and riches. You are not barely saved. You are totally saved, and with that salvation, God adds blessings. I rejoice every time I read 2 Corinthians 8:9:

> **For ye know the grace of our Lord Jesus Christ, that, though he was rich, yet for your sakes he became poor, that ye through his poverty might be rich.**

I know God wants us to be blessed. The coat of many colors represents God's many blessings, but there is a problem with wearing the coat.

The coat of many colors was taken from Joseph and torn. (Gen. 37:31.) His brothers put the blood of an animal on it. They tore it, took it to their father, and said, "We found this — we don't know what happened to your son." (Gen. 37:32.)

You see, there are problems and pressures in the walk of life. There is a problem of rejection by brethren. Sometimes your own family is not going to get along with you. Most families are not perfect. There are a lot of fathers today who are not really fathers, husbands who are not husbands, wives who are not wives, mothers who are not mothers. And there are many children who are not willing to respect their elders.

Joseph was rejected by his brethren. (Gen. 37:8.) Many of us have experienced that kind of rejection. Perhaps you have had rejection from your family, from your brothers, from your sisters. Many Christians have felt rejection from friends, neighbors, or co-workers because they named the name of Christ.

Joseph was rejected by society. He was sold into slavery. (Gen. 37:36.) He was bought by Midianites, who took him to Egypt where he was bought by Potiphar, an officer of Pharaoh, a captain of the guard. You will experience at least a certain amount of rejection in society. People whom you thought were your friends are going to become your enemies. Friendships that you thought would endure for years, and years, and years will fade away.

Joseph was rejected by his employer. (Gen. 39:20.) Potiphar's wife accused him of attempting to rape her, and he was put into Pharaoh's prison and remained there for years. Falsely accused and fired, all at the same time, things for Joseph were going from bad to worse.

Finally, Joseph was reduced to the lowest level to which he could go: confined in a dungeon. Before we find out how Joseph got out of his predicament, the cause and effects of his final destination in life, let us look at the cause and effects in your journey of life.

Why do people suffer rejection from brothers, sisters, family, society, employers?

Why do people find themselves sometimes reduced to the lowest and meanest of circumstances?

Four Reasons for Reduced Circumstances

Let me suggest four reasons why a Christian can find himself, or herself, in reduced circumstances.

The first is *self-inflicted*. Have you ever "shot yourself in the foot," figuratively speaking? I am sure you have. You did something you either thought was the right thing to do or something you knew was the wrong thing but decided to do it anyway. There is a law called "the law of cause and effect." In the Bible, it is found in Galatians 6:7:

> Be not deceived; God is not mocked: for whatsoever a man soweth, that shall he also reap. For he that soweth to his flesh shall of the flesh reap corruption; but he that soweth to the Spirit shall of the Spirit reap life everlasting.

If you sow bad seeds, you will reap a bad harvest. Tragically, in today's chaotic society, there are even some Christians who continue to make wrong choices, who fail to take charge of their lives. They "shoot themselves in the foot," and then stand around and say, "It's not my fault."

Periodically, I ask my young son, "What are you going to do in life?"

And he says, "I'm going to be rich."

I ask him, "What are you going to do to be rich?"

"I don't know, but I'm going to be rich."

"I don't think so. Son, if you don't know what you're going to do in life, you're going to be poor."

I talk to a lot of teenagers who cannot wait to get out of high school. And I tell them, you have not even started yet. You have four years of college beyond that, and an additional two years of college if you want a master's degree and another two years if you want your doctorate.

What are you going to do if you do not have an education in today's society?

What are you going to do in order to make a good living?

If you do not know, prepare yourself to be poor. And when you find yourself in poverty, do not blame society or anyone but yourself.

Actress Whoopie Goldberg lived on welfare at one time. Right now, present tense, she is rich. In fact, she hosted the Academy Awards once. She has gained respect in her field, because as a 40-year-old welfare mother, she decided that she was going to make something out of herself.

She set a goal of becoming an actress and pursued that goal. And after a few years of being extremely poor, she got her first, big break in the film, *The Color Purple*, and has become quite prominent in the entertainment field.

If that works for the world's crowd, I know it will work for God's people, because the Bible says in Psalm 5:12:

> **For thou, Lord, will bless the righteous; with favour wilt thou compass him as with a shield.**

Circumstance is the second reason why God's people have problems on their way to their destiny. First Peter 5:9 says:

> **Whom resist stedfast in the faith, knowing that the same afflictions are accomplished in your brethren that are in the world.**

Why is it that we, as God's people, think we are the only ones who have ever faced adverse circumstances? We often seem to think we are the only ones who ever get laid off. We think that we are the only people who have past-due notices on bills.

The fact is that the world is filled with people who are having the same kind of problems we are having. In fact, it would do you good to share some of your problems with someone else. Then you would discover there are people with even greater problems than you have. That is what the Bible is saying in Ecclesiastes 9:11:

> **I returned, and saw under the sun, that the race is not to the swift, nor the battle to the strong, neither yet bread to the wise, nor yet riches to men of understanding, nor yet favour to men of skill; but time and chance happeneth to them all.**

Jesus said to His disciples, "You've heard about those Galileans that the tower fell on. Do you think that happened to them because they were so sinful? Do you think they were the wickedest men of all men? They're not. They were just in the wrong place at the wrong time."

If you are in the wrong place at the wrong time, circumstances will put obstacles in your way. God may order your steps right through the middle of circumstances. Or God may use those circumstances to change your direction to cause you to go in the direction that He has ordered for your steps.

Satanic opposition is the third reason we have these little detours in life. Let me tell you a couple things about the devil:

First of all, he is not omnipresent, so quit thinking that the devil has been after you. If he has been after you, you have done us all a favor. If he is after you, he is not after the rest of us. He is a fallen cherub, an angelic being (Ezek. 28:14), and he has no more power than any other cherub has. One-third of the angels fell with him. That means two-thirds of the angels stayed true to God.

Psalm 34:7 says that the angels of the Lord encamp around them who fear God. You have an angel named Goodness on one side of you and an angel named Mercy on the other side. (Ps. 23:6.) There is precious little the devil can do to you that you do not allow him to do.

That is why the Bible says in Ephesians 4:27:

Neither give place to the devil.

The Bible also says in James 4:7:

Submit yourselves therefore to God. Resist the devil, and he will flee from you.

Romans 16:20 says:

**And the God of peace shall bruise Satan under
your feet shortly. . . .**

You need to understand that the devil is a defeated
foe; however, there is satanic opposition. There are little
devils, or demons, that will hinder you, if you allow
them to. Quit letting them. It is that simple.

My family and I live in the woods, and we had an
invader in our house one night. I heard this squeal,
and my wife yelled, "There's a mouse. Get it!"

I looked up from what I was doing and I said, "I
don't do mice. Rats, possums, I'll handle. You take care
of the little jobs."

The mouse escaped. A couple of hours later, I heard
another squeal. It was our daughter, Becka. She and
my wife went on a mouse hunt. Becka was in the bath-
room standing on the commode, where the mouse had
her cornered. Connie went in with a jar in which to catch
the mouse, because we are nice people; we do not kill
mice, we set them loose in the woods. She took her
broom and her jar and scared that little mouse to the
brink of death.

When she finally captured it, put the lid on the jar,
and brought it to me, she said, "Would you take this
out in the woods and let it go?"

I looked in that jar and that little mouse with big,
brown eyes and cute little ears was terrified. In my
mind, I pictured my youngest daughter screaming about
this little mouse. All she needed to do was step on it.
Fear is a natural reaction.

It is not just children, but a lot of grown-ups who,
if a mouse got loose in their house, would picture it running up their legs to attack them. Let me tell you

something: If you are born again, filled with the Holy Spirit, and understand who you are in Christ, you have as much power over the devils and demons of hell as we have in the natural world over a mouse. The only thing is, you do not catch the devil and turn him loose in the woods. You just step on his head.

Interpersonal relationships, or people problems, make up the fourth reason we have little detours in life. Even the apostles had "people problems." Acts 15:39 says:

> **And the contention was so sharp between them, that they departed asunder one from the other: and Barnabas took Mark, and sailed unto Cypress.**

The contention was sharp between Paul and Barnabas, so they had people problems. You are going to have people problems. Having told you all of that, let me encourage you. God said that in the midst of any detours you take on your way to His purpose for your life, He will be with you.

*As you live through reaping things you have sown,

*As God orders your steps through circumstances,

*As God orders your steps around satanic interference,

*As God brings you through those interpersonal relationships that could bring you down, He preserves you.

> **When thou passest through the waters, I will be with thee; and through the rivers, they shall not overflow thee: when thou walkest through the fire, thou shalt not be burned; neither shall the flame kindle upon thee.**
>
> **Isaiah 43:2**

Nebuchadnezzar said, "I see four men in that fiery furnace, and the fourth man looks like the Son of God."

(Dan. 3:25.)

The writer of Hebrews said:

> . . . I will never leave thee, nor forsake thee.
>
> **So that we may boldly say, The Lord is my helper, and I will not fear what man shall do unto me.**
>
> Hebrews 13:5,6

God is still God in the circumstances of life. And if you trust Him to order your steps, He will order your steps right. It did not look as if Joseph's steps were being ordered right. However, he learned what David learned and wrote in Psalm 23:4:

> **Yea, though I walk through the valley of the shadow of death, I will fear no evil: for thou art with me; thy rod and thy staff they comfort me.**

Do you want your steps ordered by God? Most of us do, and in the next chapter, I will show you how to do this.

Endnotes

[1] *Strong's,* "Hebrew-Chaldee Dictionary," p. 13, #452.

[2] *Ibid.,* p. 13, #477, #474.

[3] *Ibid.,* p. 48, #3130.

8

Ordering Your Steps To Be Ordered of God

If you follow Him, God will order your steps providentially, even when it does not seem as if He is in charge. When you are going through tough times, you must ask yourself a question: Is the sun shining when the clouds cover it? Yes, the sun still shines although you cannot see it for clouds.

When you go through adverse circumstances and situations, they do not change the fact that God has His hand on your life. That is when you have to look to Paul's words in 2 Corinthians 5:7: **We walk by faith, not by sight.**

There are times when you just walk by faith. You are not sure where God is taking you. You are not certain of why God is taking you in the direction He is taking you. You say that you believe Him, you trust Him, you have committed your way to Him, now you must say:

"God, You've got to order my steps, although I don't see where You're taking me. God, You order my steps."

That is the providence of God. That is when Romans 8:28 becomes a reality in your life:

And we know that all things work together for
good to them that love God, to them who are the called
according to his purpose.

That is why Joseph was able to say to his brothers
in Genesis 50:20, "You meant to do evil to me, but God
meant it for good. Everything I went through, God took
me through to get me where I am now."

Asuming, as most Bible scholars assume, that from
the time Joseph was thrown into the pit by his brothers
awaiting the slave traders until he was promoted
second in command to Pharaoh was about twelve or
thirteen years, from the time he was a youth of possibly
eighteen until he was thirty.[1] (Gen. 37:25 to Gen. 41:46.)

Would you trade a dozen years of pressing on and
pressing through trouble for the promise that you are
going to be promoted to the position of second in power
in the most powerful nation in the world? Think about
that one a minute.

Look at Job. Before the testing, he was rich. After
Satan tried him in every area of his life, and he remained
true to God, he was given twice as much as before. He
was twice as rich, and then he lived for many years
longer.

In fact, if you had interviewed Job at the end of his
life, he would not have told you about all of the troubles
which fill an entire book of the Bible. Job would have
said:

"God has been good to me. I am rich. God blessed
me, and things have been good. I had a few weeks of
real difficult times. And those few weeks were tough,
but as soon as they were over, God turned things
around. I don't know why. I don't understand how,
but God just turned it around. All the people who were
against me suddenly were for me. They brought me

gifts, and helped me get back on my feet. (Job 42:10-13.)

"Then God began to really bless everything I put my hand to do. And I've spent the one hundred and forty years since those hard circumstances well in my body, well in my soul, and well in my financial affairs. I have watched my great-great-grandchildren grow up. (Job 42:16.) It's been a good life."

On the other hand, the other extreme of thinking we are the only ones who have problems is thinking Christians are never to have any problems. Some Christians think they are never going to have any circumstances to deal with. They think that if they are children of God, they are going to float to heaven on "flowery beds of ease." Wrong!

Sometimes without even meaning to, Christians lie to folks who get saved. We tell them that, if they give their hearts to Jesus, everything will be all right.

One man said to me, "Before I became a Christian, everything was going along pretty smooth. When I became a Christian, all hell broke loose."

I said, "Welcome to the real world. You didn't have any problems with devils and demons while they had you. Now that they don't have you, you're a problem to them."

However, I am happy to report that in the midst of all your troubles, God still will order your steps. Psalm 75:6,7 says:

> **For promotion cometh neither from the east, nor from the west, nor from the south.**
>
> **But God is the judge: he putteth down one, and setteth up another.**

Do you believe that? There are so many people I could tell you about whom God has promoted supernaturally. In our previous church, one of our members was in the Reserves nearing his retirement. He had gone as high as he could go, because he did not have his high school diploma. He was an excellent sergeant, but he wanted to get that last rank and then retire. However, he told me that was an impossibility, because he did not have time to go back to high school to get a diploma.

I said, "That is okay. God's going to give you that rank."

Six months before his retirement, he got a call from the principal at the high school where he should have graduated. The man said that he had been going through his files and found the sergeant's diploma! The principal wanted to know if the man wanted it? Of course, he said yes, and the principal sent it.

Six weeks after the sergeant turned in his diploma, he got his promotion. Five months later, he retired with an extra $200 a month for the rest of his life. He is happy. That is promotion. God will promote you. But for God to promote you, you have to let Him order your steps.

Five "Its" to Promotion

There are five words — all ending in "it" — that, if acted on, will bring you into the place where God can order your steps: *Submit, Commit, Omit, Remit,* and *Permit*.

1. Submit yourself to God. Quit doing your thing and start doing God's thing. Amos 3:3 says, **Can two walk together, except they be agreed?** If you do not walk with God, He cannot walk with you. If you decide you want to be your own person and go your own way, God will say, "Have a nice day." He will let you do your own thing, and you will keep shooting yourself in the foot. Submit yourself to God.

You submit by saying, "Lord, not my will but Yours be done."

Submitting yourself can be scary if you are one of those people who always want to be in control. We often mistake the feeling of control for the feeling of security. The truth is that there is no greater security in our lives than knowing God is in control.

2. Commit to follow Jesus. First John 1:7 says,

If we walk in the light, as he is in the light, we have fellowship one with another, and the blood of Jesus Christ his Son cleanseth us from all sin.

Not are you only submitted to God, you are committed to God. You are going to follow Him. You are going to do right things. That is righteousness. You are going to live a lifestyle pleasing to God. Are you committed?

3. Omit a negative lifestyle from your life. Do not go out every Saturday night to party, party, party, come to church with a hangover on Sunday morning, and expect God to bless you. Yes, we need to understand that "who the Son has set free is free indeed" (John 8:36). But there are some folks who are just too free. Romans 8:1 says:

There is therefore now no condemnation to them which are in Christ Jesus, who walk not after the flesh, but after the Spirit.

I was preaching one Sunday in a church that Connie and I pastored previously when, for some reason or other I got onto the subject of fornication. I made it plain and embarrassed a few people.

A young lady came up to me after service and said, "No condemnation. No condemnation."

If she had not done that, I would not have known what she had been doing.

I looked at her and said, "Sis, some people just need a little condemnation."

What I meant, of course, is that some people need to feel conviction over their sins. Without conviction, there is no true repentance. *Condemnation* is simply remorse, guilt, and shame. It does not bring repentance and a changed lifestyle.

Many people get caught up in negative lifestyles, which suck them under in one of life's undertows. Keep yourself from God's best, and it may ultimately lead you out from underneath His grace. Then you are in a world of trouble. Omit your negative lifestyle.

4. Remit to God what belongs to God. Psalm 50:14,15 says:

> Offer unto God thanksgiving; and pay thy vows unto the most High:
>
> And call upon me in the day of trouble: I will deliver thee, and thou shalt glorify me.

We looked at Malachi 3:10 in the last chapter, where God made it plain about bringing the tithe into His storehouse. I am sure that someone reading this book will immediately think, "All these preachers ever talk about is money," but I will give you a biblical prospective. *If God does not have your money, He does not have you.*

Do not tell me you are submitted to God, committed to God, omitting a negative lifestyle, if you are not remitting to God what He said belongs to Him.

Do not tell me God is going to order your steps to prosperity and blessing, if you are not faithful in your tithes and in your offerings.

If you give God what belongs to Him, then God will prosper you. I believe this, and I have proved it true in my own life. Remit to God what is His, and God will bless you.

5. Permit God to intervene in your life.

I know a family who was thinking about attending our church, because something about this church impressed them — nobody dies. That is not to say people do not die at our church, because they do. We have funerals once in a while, but not on a large percentile basis. We just keep people around. We have not had a funeral in our church for about nine months. That is not average for a church this size.

There are churches which expect to have a funeral every week. We do not believe in funerals. I would rather see people healed and blessed. It does make a difference what you hear, what you believe, and what you apply in your life. You need God on your side. More than that, you need to get on God's side. Give God an invitation to intervention.

If you are not a Christian, and you want to permit God to intervene in your life, pray this prayer:

"Lord, save me. Forgive me of my sins. Change my life. Make me what You want me to be."

And if you are a Christian who has been messing around, dilly-dallying, and not pursuing God the way that you should, you need to pray, "Lord, order my steps." Second Chronicles 16:9 says:

> **For the eyes of the Lord run to and fro throughout the whole earth, to shew himself strong in behalf of them whose heart is perfect toward him . . . .**

Do not let that word *perfect* scare you.

Do not say that God will never order your steps because you are not perfect. The word translated *perfect* in that verse is the Hebrew word, shalem, which means "complete (lit. or fig.); especially friendly: — full, just, made ready, peaceable, whole."[2]

The eyes of the Lord are running to and fro right now, looking for someone who is whole toward Him. God can show Himself strong in your behalf because you are His friend through the blood covenant cut on your behalf by Jesus. (Heb. 8:6.)

If you were to die right now, where would you go? Heaven or hell? Are you certain of your eternity?

If you are reading this book, and your steps have not been directed by God, you need to make certain that your steps are directed by God.

Jesus wants to touch you. His eyes are going up and down across the earth right now, looking for someone who will be a friend to Him. He is calling you.

Pray with me:

> *Lord, in the name of Jesus, as I pray, I bind principalities and powers. Father, I believe the price Jesus paid on Calvary was sufficient to purchase redemption and to make it a reality so that You could order my steps for good. I am tired of struggling on my own. Thank You, Lord, for doing the work. Amen.*

Endnotes

[1] Boone, R. Jerome. *The New Chronological Bible* (World Bible Publishers, Copyright E. E. Gaddy & Assoc., 1980), pp. 94, 100. Years given are 1865 B.C. to 1852 B.C.

[2] *Strong's*, p. 117, #8003.

9

Seven Life Lessons for Success

In the late eighties, when the religious scandals were going on, someone said to me, "We're going to have you followed. We want to find out what you're doing."

I said, "Help yourself," and I thought that someone was about to be bored out of his mind.

I am the same when I get up in the morning as I am when I go to bed. From one day to the next day, I am predictable. Even in my unpredictability, I am predictable. I live a stable, balanced, and moderate life.

Those are three concepts you will see all through this chapter. The first concept is *stability*. In Romans 16:25, the Apostle Paul wrote, **Now to him that is of power to stablish you according to my gospel.**

The second concept is *balance*. Solomon wrote in Proverbs 16:11, **A just weight and balance are the Lord's.**

The third concept is *moderation*. Philippians 4:5 says, **Let your moderation be known to all men. The Lord is at hand.**

You may think these three concepts — stability, balance, and moderation — make a really boring life.

However, before you write them off, look at Revelation 21:9,10 where John the Revelator tells of being visited by an angel.

> **And there came unto me one of the seven angels . . . saying, Come hither, I will shew thee the bride, the Lamb's wife.**
>
> **And he carried me away in the spirit to a great and high mountain, and shewed me that great city, the holy Jerusalem, descending out of heaven from God.**

In verse 16, the angel said, **The city lieth four-square**, which means that the city was a square. The length and the breadth and the height of it are equal. It was described as a perfectly square cube. Do we really think Jesus is married to a city?

Some Bible prophecy teachers insist that a 1500-square-mile city is going to drop out of heaven when Jesus returns, and that is going to be the center of the Kingdom of God on planet earth. That just does not fit biblically, nor does it make practical sense.

The atmosphere of the earth is only ten miles thick, which means one thousand, four hundred and ninety miles of that city would be in the vacuum of outer space. If the Bride is a literal city of that literal size, you had better hope you get a condo on the lower floor!

You see, the Bride of Christ is not a city in the sense of a physical city. The Bride of Christ is the Church. We are the New Jerusalem, the City of God. Hebrews 12:22 says:

> **But ye are come unto mount Sion, and unto the city of the living God, the heavenly Jerusalem, and to an innumerable company of angels.**

To understand the symbology, you need to get a picture in your mind of this heavenly Jerusalem being four-square, with 1200 furlongs on one side, 1200 on the other side, and 1200 high: perfectly balanced.

In Exodus 37:1, we read about the ark of the covenant being made "two and a half cubits long, a cubit and a half wide, and a cubit and a half high." And it was overlaid with pure gold within and without and had a crown of gold round about it. In other words, it was balanced.

Numbers 8:2 says:

> Speak unto Aaron, and say unto him, When thou lightest the lamps, the seven lamps shall give light over against the candlestick.

The original candlestick in the tabernacle was made out of one piece of beaten gold. It had seven lamps on it, and the seven lamps that gave light were balanced. Everything God used in the tabernacle and temple not only had a literal purpose in Old Testament times, but each item was a symbol or type of the spiritual Kingdom to begin on earth when Jesus came. (Matt. 4:17.)

If you have the three concepts of *balance, stability,* and *motivation* in your life, it will be pleasing to God and acceptable to man. You will make it to heaven and take some people with you. Having established all of that, let me give you those seven lessons for everyday living.

Seven Life Lessons

1. Life Is a Journey — Prepare for It.

The first lesson is that life is a journey, prepare for it. You must start where you are in order to get where you are going. Third John 2 says:

> Beloved, I wish above all things that thou mayest prosper and be in health, even as thy soul prospereth.

The Greek word *enodoo* is only translated prosper once in the New Testament. It means "to succeed in business affairs," but it also means "to (have a) prosper (ous) journey."[1] You have to prepare for your journey through life, which is ongoing.

If you are going to prosper and be in health as your soul prospers (your mind, your will, and your intellect), you must watch your attitude. That is part of your preparation.

If you are going to prosper, that means you need to get an education.

If you are going to prosper, you need to have expectation. That is part of your preparation.

If you want to make it to the end of the journey, if you want success on the journey, and understand that life is a journey, you have to prepare for it.

2. Each Stage Is Different — Experience It.

Each stage of life is different, take time to experience it. Sometimes you get into such a big hurry to get on with the rest of your life, you miss the best part of today. If life is a journey, each stage is different, so experience it one day at a time. Live life to the fullest.

Paul said in Philippians 4:11:

> **Not that I speak in respect of want: for I have learned, in whatsoever state I am, therewith to be content.**

I also have learned how to live with little, and I know how to live with abundance. Whatever state I am in, I am content, because I know that God orders my steps.

When we were first married, Connie and I were really, really poor. There were people who thought we would never stay married because we were so poor, but we really enjoyed life. We did not have any better sense than to enjoy it. We were young, out preaching the Gospel, doing what God called us to do, and we enjoyed it. We have prospered and grown since those days. We have been through some tough times and good times, but we have experienced contentment in all of our times.

Each stage is different, experience it.

3. Relationships Require Effort — Expend It.

Do you want friends? Proverbs 18:24 says that a person who has friends must show himself friendly. That does not mean walking up to someone after church and saying, "My name is . . . what is your name? Let's be friends."

Friendship requires an effort, which means you have to get to know that person, not just visit two hours on Sunday morning. You have to expend effort to have friends.

Are you making an effort to have friends? Out of those friendships, you will develop a few choice relationships. Relationships take even more effort than friendships. Relationships require effort, expend it.

4. Have a Vocation — Find It.

There is something in life that you will enjoy doing — find it. My son John and I were driving up the interstate a few years ago and, up to that point in his life, he did not like to work. He did not like doing his chores or working at anything. But it is a rule in the Stutzman family that, when you reach 13 years old, you go to work in the church office. (I pay my children myself, and they have flexible hours.) We want them to learn to work and to learn to be responsible.

At any rate, driving up the interstate this particular day, John said, "Dad, I've come to this realization. I've decided that if I have work to do, I'm going to get it done and get it out of the way, so that I can do what I want to do."

What a revelation! And it must have been a revelation to John, because ever since then, when he has had work to do, he has done it. He has gotten it out of the way so that he could be free to do what he wanted to do. Then, he found a job working for someone else. Now, he likes to work. He works all of the time and enjoys what he does.

There is something you can do in life which you will enjoy. And, when you are doing what you like doing, it is no longer work. First Thessalonians 4:11 says:

> **And that ye study to be quiet, and to do your own business, and to work with your own hands, as we commanded you.**

If you do not enjoy what you are doing, you need to find something that you will enjoy doing. If you have to get some extra education to do that thing, if you have to learn techniques to accomplish that thing, then do it, and God will bless you in the process. When you are doing what you like to do, it is not work anymore.

Someone asked me one time how I keep up with my schedule.

I replied, "I'm having a blast. I am enjoying myself. Even in the aggravations, even dealing with people's problems and frustrations, I'm having a good time because I've found my vocation."

Find your vocation, and you will enjoy what you do in life.

5. God Has a Purpose for You — Fulfill It.

God does have a purpose for you. You are not an accident waiting to happen, you have purpose. Second Timothy 1:9 says:

> **Who hath saved us, and called us with an holy calling, not according to our works, but according to his own purpose and grace, which was given us in Christ Jesus before the world began.**

God has called you with a purpose. He has an eternal purpose, which is for you and me to rule and reign in eternity with Christ. That is your eternal purpose. There are temporal purposes God has for your life as well. God put you where He put you for a purpose.

Some of you are working at a job that God put you in as a mission field.

Some of you are living in neighborhoods that God has put you in as a mission field. Proverbs 11:30 tells us that he who "wins souls is wise." There are eternal purposes, and there are temporal purposes. God has a purpose for your life.

Fulfill God's purpose in your life, and you will see two things happen: You will see God move actively in your natural life, and you will see God move supernaturally in your life. In the eternities, you will see a great reward. God has a purpose for you.

6. Time Is a Treasure, Guard It.

Do not let the time bandits steal your time. Most people do not think about time. You will never get back the minutes you spend. So if you waste them, you ought to waste them on purpose, not because some time bandit has come along and stolen those minutes away from you. Ephesians 5:16 says, **Redeeming the time, because the days are evil.**

There are people who say, "Well, I just don't have enough time."

Wrong; they have plenty of time. It is just that most people never think enough about managing their time. There is an old saying that "time is money." It is. It is also *like* money.

If you do not manage your money, you will never accumulate it. If you do not manage your time, you will never have enough time. Time is a treasure, guard it.

7. Wisdom is a Principal Thing — Get It.

Wisdom is applied knowledge. Wisdom used to be called common sense. Older generations called it "horse sense," because a horse by nature will do what is best for it. Society has very little horse sense, very little common sense, and very little wisdom. Proverbs 4:7 states:

> **Wisdom is the principal thing; therefore get wisdom: and with all thy getting get understanding.**

According to 1 Corinthians 1:30, Jesus is the personification of wisdom to us, as well as salvation, sanctification, and righteousness:

> **But of him are ye in Christ Jesus, who of God is made unto us wisdom, and righteousness, and sanctification, and redemption.**

Jesus has become your wisdom, and if you are filled with the Spirit of Christ and led by the Spirit of Christ, you can personify the wisdom of Christ. Get wisdom.

Before you take any action, ask yourself, "What's going to be the effect of this action?"

Before you shoot yourself in the foot, ask yourself, "Will this hurt? Will this keep me from running the race?"

One of my uncles has told me about a time when he was a kid and had a real curiosity about how fast a BB shot came out of the barrel of a gun. He kept thinking about that. One day he decided to find out. So he powered up his air rifle, stuck his thumb over the barrel, and pulled the trigger. He found out how fast the shot came out of the gun by shooting himself in the thumb!

If he had exercised a little wisdom, he could have read the instruction manual and found out the speed of a BB shot, but he did what a lot of us do. He never read the instruction manual and had to learn the hard way.

You know what wisdom does? Wisdom learns from the mistakes of others. Wisdom learns from observation.

One of the problems with the Charismatic/Pentecostal movement is that many people want excitement more than wisdom or understanding. They want to be excited. I too like excitement. I like exciting worship services. I believe in miracles, and at our church, we see miracles on a regular basis.

However, more than miracles, I am interested in seeing people get where they are going. I am not interested in excitement just to be excited and in a shout just to be shouting. Without the seven principles above, the spiritual becomes a life of ups and downs, temporary excitement followed by depression. That is not a stable

Christian life, which leads to God-ordered steps. We must be planted in Jesus to be stable in our walk.

In the next chapter, I want to give you seven secrets to being able to walk in stability. If you put them into practice along with the seven principles in this chapter, they will enable you to begin to have victory in Jesus.

Endnotes

[1]*Strong's*, "Greek Dictionary," p. 33, #2137.

10
Seven Secrets of Stability

In 1 Corinthians 16:13, the Apostle Paul was wrapping up some advice to the church at Corinth, and there are seven points in that verse that become keys to stability.

Watch ye, stand fast in the faith, quit you like men, be strong.

The first "secret," or practical hint, is stay awake. That is what the word *watch* means. Stay awake. Watch with vigilance. In 1 Thessalonians 5:6, Paul was writing again about an attitude of vigilance:

Therefore let us not sleep, as do others; but let us watch and be sober.

Vigilance means to watch and stay awake. Temptation is going to come your way. Have you ever suffered temptation? Well, if you have your eyes closed, if you are sleeping when temptation comes your way, it is going to take you.

Watch. Jesus told His disciples, watch and pray. Somewhere along the line people have the idea that if they pray, they are supposed to close their eyes. No, you keep one eye open because you do not know what is coming down the pike. Keep one eye open, figuratively speaking, even while you are praying. Stay awake.

The Apostle Peter also warned Christians to be alert. He wrote in 1 Peter 5:8:

> **Be sober, be vigilant; for your adversary the devil, as a roaring lion, walketh about, seeking whom he may devour.**

The scripture tells us that we are to "gird up the loins of our mind."

We are to watch.

We are to stay awake.

We are to be vigilant.

The second secret of stability is stand fast. The word in the Greek is "be stationary."[1] Persevere.

The old-time Pentecostals put it like this, "You've got to keep on keeping on."

We live in a generation that wants to give up or turn back when it faces adversities. If you want to be stable, stand fast. Proverbs 24:10 says:

> **If thou faint in the day of adversity, thy strength is small.**

There is a well-known secular motivational saying that has a lot of truth in it: "Quitters never win and winners never quit."

Every successful person in life has failed at least once before making it. Henry Ford went bankrupt three times before he developed the Ford automobile. Thomas Alva Edison tried a thousand different filaments for the incandescent light before he finally came up on a piece of carbonized thread. Success is littered with failure. You will never succeed until you face some failures.

The key to winning, however, is that in the midst of failure, you do not turn back — you just stand.

If God plants you in a church, stay where you are and work for the success of that church, whether you like everything going on there or not.

If God gives you a good job, stay where you are even if there is some persecution or even if you do not quite like it. Only leave for something else if God leads you to do so.

If God gives you a good wife, a good husband, stay where you are and keep on doing what you are doing — if it is working. If it is not, seek the Lord as to what you are doing wrong or not doing that you should be and change your ways. Do not run from your marriage problems and go looking for greener fields. You will only take your same old problems into the new situation.

The third secret is quit you like men. Those are four words in the English language that describe one Greek word, *andrizomai*, that means "to act manly."[2] That is not a sexist statement, although it applies to both men and women in the Lord. The idea is "to be strong and stable."

When you do that, you are exhibiting "manly" characteristics. You are not whining childishly over the ball life throws you. Instead you are standing over the plate with a heart to win the game. Stop whining and start winning.

The Church Is Not a Social Agency

Once in a while, a person will come to me and say, "Pastor, I'm leaving the church because I haven't made any friends," or "Pastor, I'm leaving the church because, well, I'm looking for a spouse and I have not found one here."

Or they will say, "Pastor, I'm leaving the church because I had a $958 telephone bill, and the church would not help me with it."

Perhaps someone will say, "Pastor, I'm leaving the church because one Sunday morning, you preached about people who were whining instead of winning (or some other wrong attitude or sin), and nobody's going to preach to me that way."

Of course, the person who says that automatically marks himself or herself as being or doing whatever it was the Holy Spirit led me to preach on. What that means is that the person would not accept correction from the Holy Spirit and wants to be let alone in their sins.

Let me tell you four things God did *not* establish the Church to be:

1. God did not invent the Church to be a dating service, or to provide a place for you to build relationships. People ought to, can, and do form relationships in churches, but that cannot be their main motivation for attending.

2. God did not make the Church to be a bank or welfare system. If people have emergencies, most churches try to help out. However, the Church is not your source; God is your source. A church is not going to finance your car, pay off your credit cards, or buy your Easter suit. By the way, our church staff and some of the members have been approached on all of the above at one time or another.

3. God intended the Church to be a place where you can work for Him and where He can work on you. That is why God intended for the Church to be a conduit into which you, as an independent believer, could get plugged in and find some area of ministry. It

might be ministry to the Body of Christ or ministry to the outside world.

4. Jesus never intended for the Church to be a social agency. Jesus did intend for the Church to be an agency that would affect social change through being the "light of the world." (Matt. 5:14,15.) And, my friend, there is a great difference between being a social agency that people go to for help with problems in society and being an agency that changes society to deal with the problems.

If you are looking for the Church to fulfill all the inadequacies of your life, you will be sadly disappointed. The inadequacies of your life can only be addressed by one person, and that is you. Stop whining. When the Israelites did that on the trip out of Egypt, God called it "grumbling and complaining." When they did not stop, it cost them the Promised Land.

The fourth secret is be strong. The Greek word for *strong* is *krataioo*, which means "to empower" or "to increase with vigor."[3] In Ephesians 6:10, Paul wrote to **be strong in the Lord, and in the power of his might**. It is easy to be strong. You can be as strong as you want to be.

Every year at Christmas, Connie and I buy a family gift, one that we want as well as the children and one all of us can use. A couple of years ago, we bought a nice home gym. It sits downstairs at our house, and I walk by it every day.

Occasionally I say to myself, "I need to work out."

I have found that if I say that every day for seven days, I will work out. When I am in one of my workout phases, I work out diligently — at least twice.

See, it is simple to stay in shape physically, but it is not always easy. All you have to do is exercise. All you have to do is cut back on the junk food. And it is simple to stay in shape spiritually. Isaiah 40:31 says;

> **But they that wait upon the Lord shall renew their strength; they shall mount up with wings as eagles; they shall run, and not be weary; and they shall walk, and not faint.**

How To Stay Spiritually Strong

It is simple to stay strong spiritually. All you have to do is cut out the spiritual junk food. Get yourself in the Word of God. Spend some time waiting on God and you will renew your strength. You will mount up on wings as eagles, run and not be weary, and walk and not faint

Be strong in the Lord and in the power of His might. Spend some time waiting on God; in fact, spend some time every day waiting on God. You set aside time for your job. You set aside time for your hobbies. You set aside time for your wife, your husband, and your children, and you set aside time for everything else. How much more should you set aside time to wait on God?

The fifth secret is to love out of a pure heart. Let everything you do be done with charity, with love. If you want to be strong and stable, love out of a pure heart. Loving out of a pure heart means, in essence, to love without expecting anything in return. Paul wrote about love to the church at Corinth.

> **Though I speak with the tongues of men and of angels, and have not charity, I am become as sounding brass, or a tinkling cymbal.**
>
> **1 Corinthians 13:1**

Charity is used in the *King James Version* of the Bible to translate *agape,* the Greek word which means "unconditional love, affection or benevolence."[4] We might say the "God-kind" of love. The original word did not mean sexual love in any shape or form. The Greek word for sexual or marital love is *eros.*

Our society equates love with sentimentality and romance or with *eros,* with a cute little cherub (which is unscriptural in its appearance) who shoots arrows at people causing them to "fall in love" or "fall in lust" (one or the other). That is why people get married for the wrong reasons.

That is not the love that Paul was talking about. That is not pure love. That is love which gives in order to get that type of love in return. To be stable, love out of a pure heart.

Then there is this concept in our society that, "If you loved me, you wouldn't talk to me like that. You would not correct me, or tell me strong truths."

We have this idea that if you love people you let them do whatever they want to do. That is not unconditional, pure love; that is unconditional permissiveness. A perfect example is in the area of parenting.

Parents, the best thing you can ever do for your children is to correct them with love. The Bible says that if God does not "chastise" (correct or convict) you, really you are not His child. (Heb. 12:8.)

Society is in a mess today because there are many children who have grown up without the real love of a parent. In the majority of cases in the last forty years, children either have been reared permissively or abusively. Either way is an extreme and wrong. Real love corrects when necessary without being abusive.

Love out of a pure heart. A man named Stephanas is an example of one who did this in the early Church. Stephanas means "crowned Christian."[5] You want to be a strong, stable, balanced Christian.

> **I beseech you, brethren, (ye know the house of Stephanas, that it is the firstfruits of Achaia, and that they have *addicted* themselves to the ministry of the saints,)**
>
> **That ye submit yourselves unto such, and to every one that helpeth with us, and laboureth.**
>
> **1 Corinthians 16:15,16**

Stephanas is an illustration. He was "a crowned Christian," and he and his household were addicted to the ministry of the saints. The Greek word translated *addicted* in that verse does not mean "addiction" in the sense that we think of addiction. It means "to arrange in an orderly manner, to decide or to dispose."[6]

Stephanas had his life in order and was ministering to the needs of the saints. He was being "a servant to the saints," which is what the word *ministry* — *diakoneo* in the Greek — means.[7] He was a deacon to the saints, a crowned Christian. His life was in order; therefore, he was ministering to the saints.

Order Flows Through Proper Authority

That brings us to our sixth point: Set yourself in order. Submit. Paul said, in reference to Stephanas, that Christians are to submit to everyone who helps us and labors. There are a great number of military people in my church. I love military people because military people understand order. They understand private and general, and all of the ranks in between.

You can go all through the New Testament and find reference after reference where the Church is equated to an army. I have never seen a good military person who walked out of order. That does not mean they always agree with those over them. That does not mean they do not express disagreement at times. However, once everything is said and done, the smoke clears, and decisions made, they submit and walk in order. The Church could learn a few things from the military way.

Hebrews 13:17 is a major biblical doctrine.

> **Obey them that have the rule over you, and submit yourselves: for they watch for your souls, as they that must give account, that they may do it with joy, and not with grief: for that is unprofitable for you.**

Jesus endorsed this concept, and He lived by it Himself. He only did what He "saw" the Father do (John 5:19) and said, **Not my will, but thine, be done,** even when it came to crucifixion. (Luke 22:42.) There are many other instances in Scripture of Jesus being submitted to authority over Him, including His parents. (Luke 2:51.) He submitted to earthly authorities by paying the exorbitant temple and Roman taxes. (Matt. 17:27.)

Remember the Roman centurion who came to Jesus on behalf of his servant? Remember that Jesus said He had not found faith like that man's in all Israel? (Luke 7:9.) What an indictment of the Jewish people who heard Jesus preach!

The Roman's faith was stable *because he understood authority* and submitted to it.

The centurion's servant was healed because the centurion understood the concept of order.

The word *obey* means "to assent (to evidence or authority)" or in modern terms, "to set yourself under" someone or some authority.[8]

When you find godly leadership that is led by the Spirit of God and a church that is strong, stable and growing, then suddenly everything seems wrong to you, you may need to check yourself. Any time a church moves up and makes changes, there are a certain number of folks who get uncomfortable.

On the other hand, everything you see on Christian television or in churches is not necessarily the move of God.

Someone once said everyone ought to fall out in a specific section when you point to it under the anointing. I love seeing people "slain in the Spirit." It happens all of the time in my meetings, but I am much more interested in seeing people "stand" than fall.

When God sets order in the church, follow after that order. Do not let some weird or minor thing blow you out of the house of God. There are only four reasons I can see why a person ought to ever leave a church, once God plants him in it:

*If you are not being fed, you ought to go where you will be fed. You may not always like what you get fed, but you do get fed.

*If you get abused from the pulpit so that you feel worse when the service is over than when you came in, that is a good reason to leave. I am not talking about being preached under conviction; I am talking about feeling bruised and beaten in your spirit.

*If God speaks to you to leave, and you know it is God. In that case, there is a right way to leave and a wrong way.

The right way is to go to your pastor and go to the elders and tell them you think God is speaking to you to go somewhere else. If it is God moving you, and if your leadership is in the right place with God, you will get a confirmation.

The wrong way to leave is to just disappear or to begin to talk about the church, saying there must be something wrong because God is pulling you out. Above all, do not take anyone else with you!

*If you move geographically, you have a reason to change churches.

Those are the only four reasons, biblically, I can find for anyone to move from one church to another church. If God has planted you in a church, do not allow yourself to be shaken by anything there. Remain stable. Submit.

The seventh secret of stability is to be a supporter. If you want to be strong, if you want to be stable, if you want to be balanced, if you want to live a life of moderation, be a supporter. I read a book by a motivational speaker written from a purely secular standpoint. Yet it had one chapter devoted entirely to tithing.

The author did not have a biblical concept of a tithe as supporting the house of God, but he did have the biblical concept of the tithe as in the giving the "tenth." I was really interested to find a secular motivational speaker telling his constituency they needed to take 10 percent of their money and put it somewhere besides themselves.

His rationale was that, in doing this, you are saying to yourself, "I have everything I need and enough left over to give away 10 percent of it."

In tithing, you are making an affirmation to yourself. As you tithe you are not even tithing into a church. The church is simply a depository. You are tithing into the eternal Kingdom of God. The New Testament says that, under the old covenant, God's people tithed to an earthly priest, but in the new covenant, we tithe to Jesus. (Heb. 7:8.)

If you want to be strong, if you want to be stable, if you want to be balanced, be a supporter of the work of God. In Philippians 4:16,17,19, Paul wrote:

> **Even in Thessalonica ye sent once and again unto my necessity.**

> **Not because I desire a gift: but I desire fruit that may abound to your account.**

> **But my God shall supply all your need according to his riches in glory by Christ Jesus.**

If you are a tither and a giver, you will be balanced. Your finances will become stable. One of our elders recently talked to me about tithing and sowing. He said everything good God has done in his life financially is because he has paid his tithes and sowed seeds. Tithing works in his life because he is stable and consistent in it.

Stability is a wonderful thing. When you are stable, God brings increase into your life, year by year. You will move from one blessing to another blessing, and you will carry others into the blessing.

Endnotes

[1] *Strong's*, "Greek Dictionary," P. 38, #2476.
[2] *Ibid.*, p. 12, #407.
[3] *Ibid.*, p. 43, #2901.
[4] *Ibid.*, p. 7, #26.
[5] *Ibid.*, p. 66, #4734.
[6] *Ibid.*, p. 71, #5021.
[7] *Ibid.*, p. 22, 1247.
[8] *Ibid.*, p. 56, 3982.

11
God-Ordered Relationships: Love and Marriage

A movie made of the life of pop singer Tina Turner a couple of years ago had a title that summed up her marital experiences: *What's Love Got to Do With It?* The title song was another hit for her. In a nation where half of all marriages end in divorce, the song's title is a good question.

Years ago, Nancy Sinatra and Lee Hazelwood phrased society's idea about "love" from the same perspective in a country song, "I'm Going to Jackson," about a couple who got married "in a fever hotter than a pepper sprout."

There is a godly order for marriage. Unfortunately, God's order is not the reason most people get married. Too often people get married for the wrong reasons. People get married because they are in L-O-V-E, which is probably the second worst reason for getting married. The worst reason for getting married is a pregnancy.

Connie and I have been married for more than twenty years. I have never, nor has she ever, forgotten our anniversary. She is not only my wife, but also my best friend. She is cute, intelligent, and I love her a lot. I buy her roses on occasion. I remember her birthday. I open and shut the car door for her. I try to make sure she is dressed reasonably well. I want to make certain that you understand how I treat my wife, because as you read this chapter, you might mistakenly think that I am a mean, unromantic man.

A woman came up to Connie years ago and said, "Oh, it must be wonderful to be married to a great man of God."

My wife said, "Yeah, right. The great man of God is just as grouchy as your husband before he has his second cup of coffee in the morning."

In Ephesians 5:21, Paul establishes our relationships within the Body of Christ, **Submitting yourselves one to another in the fear of God**, then he moves right on into discussing the marriage relationship in verses 22-25.

> **Wives, submit yourselves unto your own husbands, as unto the Lord.**
>
> **For the husband is the head of the wife, even as Christ is the head of the church: and he is the saviour of the body.**
>
> **Therefore as the church is subject unto Christ, so let the wives be to their own husbands in every thing.**
>
> **Husbands, love your wives, even as Christ also loved the church, and gave himself for it.**

These are God's standards for marriage in any time and any society. Paul speaks to wives and tells them to submit themselves. The word *submit*, from the Greek word *hupotasso*, means "to obey," "to be subordinate to," or "to submit oneself unto."[1] Women may think that is a rather stringent requirement, particularly in today's climate, but requirements on men are just as stringent.

God's requirement for a husband is, "Husbands, love your wives — but not with the hero's kind of love, not with the sexual love, and not with the friendship kind of love. Husbands, love your wives with agape love, the kind of love that God exhibited to us through His only Son — a sacrificial love."

In fact, husbands are instructed by the Word of God to love their wives as Christ loved the Church and gave Himself for it. The word *gave* means "to surrender."[2] As Christ gave Himself up for the Church, husbands are to give themselves up for their wives.

Paul was not the only apostle to write this way. There is a parallel in Peter's first epistle. First Peter 3:1 states:

> **Likewise, ye wives, be in subjection to your own husbands; that, if any obey not the word, they also may without the word be won by the conversation of the wives.**

If you are a woman who has a problem with this, find a husband who wants a boss. Or, find a husband who wants a mother. There are a few men out there looking for their "mommies," and they will gladly allow their wives to mother them. Of course, most women do not enjoy being surrogate mothers, they want a husband who is a husband.

If you still have a problem with Paul's instructions, just do not get married at all. There really are some people who ought not to be married, both men and women.

Things That Hinder Your Prayers

I am "equal opportunity," so let us hear what Peter has to say to men. In verse seven, he says:

> **Likewise, ye husbands, dwell with them accord-**
> **ing to knowledge, giving honour unto the wife, as**
> **unto the weaker vessel, and as being heirs together**
> **of the grace of life; that your prayers be not hindered.**

Men, if you do not honor your wives, God is not going to honor you. You are going to pray prayers that will never be answered if you do not honor your wives — **That your prayers be not hindered**. If you are not walking in authority yourself, you have no authority. If you are not living as the head of the house, you have no authority.

Do not say you are the head of the house, if you are not leading your house in the ways of God.

Do not say you are the head of the house, if you are not a man of the Word and a man of prayer.

If you are not a man of prayer, you have abdicated your responsibility as the head of the house. You may say you work hard at your job and are too tired to pray, but in today's society, your wife probably works hard at a job. Society's obligations do not negate spiritual responsibility.

Spiritual authority only comes when you have set yourself under authority according to the principles we see in the centurion's story in Matthew 8:8,9.

We see a good example in Genesis 24 of a person operating in authority because he was totally submitted to authority. At that point, Abraham was an old man, and his son Isaac was still unmarried. He did not want his son to marry one of the Canaanite women in whose land they are dwelling. So, he sent his most trusted servant, who is unnamed in the Bible, back to Haran in Mesopotamia to find a bride for Isaac.

The reason for this was that Abraham's brother Nahor and his children had remained in the land of

Haran when Abram (his original name) moved on to Canaan. When Abram, his father, and the rest of the family left Ur of the Chaldees, they settled for a while in Haran. Abraham knew he still had relatives there. (Gen. 11:31,32.)

In Genesis 24:4, we read:

> **But thou shalt go unto my country, and to my kindred, and take a wife unto my son Isaac.**

The unnamed servant traveled to Haran, and there, he prayed to "the God of Abraham" for a sign to help him find the right girl.

In essence, he prayed, "Let me find favor with You, Lord. When I come to Haran, let the first woman I see at the village well offer to draw water for my camels when I ask her to get me a drink. (vv. 13,14.)

The first woman to appear was named Rebekah, and he asked her to give him a drink of water. When he received the water, she told him that she also would draw water for his camels. (vv. 18,19.) The servant had ten camels. The 22nd verse says:

> **And it came to pass, as the camels had done drinking, that the man took a golden earring of half a shekel weight, and two bracelets for her hands of ten shekels weight of gold.**

Then he asked whose daughter she was and if he could spend the night at their home. The servant found that God had given him a sign: She was the granddaughter of Abraham's brother. Also, she invited him to stay at her house. This was before she knew who he was. (vv. 23-25.)

He gave her the jewelry and went to her home. There he introduced himself to her mother and brother as the servant of their kinsman, whom the Lord had blessed greatly with "flocks and herds, silver and gold, menservants, maidservants, camels and asses." (vv. 34,35.)

After he shared with them all of the details (vv. 36-48) about his assignment, his prayer, and how the Lord had answered, he said:

> **And now if ye will deal kindly and truly with my master, tell me: and if not, tell me; that I may turn to the right hand, or to the left.**
>
> **Then Laban and Bethuel answered and said, The thing proceedeth from the Lord: we cannot speak unto thee bad or good.**
>
> **Behold, Rebekah is before thee, take her and go, and let her be thy master's son's wife, as the Lord hath spoken.**
>
> **Verses 49-51**

This was an *arranged marriage*. How many of us would accept an arranged marriage? How many parents would like to have arranged their children's marriages?

The servant wanted to leave immediately. He wanted to quickly complete this errand, probably the most important he had ever been given. He wanted to get the girl back to his master once he found she and her family were willing. Her family wanted him to wait at least ten days before he left, because of the suddenness of events.

However, Abraham's servant could not stand to wait, and Rebekah was willing, so they left very soon. The rest of that chapter tells of Isaac being out in the fields meditating the evening the caravan returned. Rebekah got off her camel to meet him, and Isaac took her into his tent as his wife. Scripture tells us that he *loved* her and was "comforted" after his mother's death. (vv. 52-67.)

Ten Reasons To Marry and Stay Married

Out of this amazing story, we can find ten good reasons to get married and to stay married. If you are going to be married, you need to be married for the right reasons.

1. Do not marry for love, marry for like.

Psychologists say that "fluttery feeling" which most people call love lasts about six months. Unfortunately, many of you reading this book probably were married during those first six months. Then, one morning you woke up, the fluttery feeling was gone, and you asked yourself why you married your spouse. You discovered you had married someone whom you did not like.

Love may flutter out the window, but like always lasts. Isaac's name means "laughter." Rebekah's name means "fettering (by beauty)."[3] These are admirable qualities in the person you are going to choose to be a husband or a wife.

Women, find someone who makes you laugh. Proverbs tells us in 17:22 that "a merry heart" is like a medicine for our good, but that "a broken spirit" dries up the bones. If you marry someone who makes you laugh, your marriage is going to last. Marry someone who lifts you up instead of puts you down. If you are married to someone with these qualities, you ought to thank God.

Men, find someone who "fetters" you by her beauty, and that does not always mean outward appearances. A woman who is beautiful inwardly will make your marriage happy. Proverbs 31 describes a beautiful woman. Marry someone who makes you look good.

People who see a man married to a woman like the one in Proverbs 31, whose ways are beautiful and who always does him good, will think that man must be a worthwhile man.

Marry someone who makes you look good. You cannot help but like that kind of person.

Marry for like, because like lasts. I like my wife. We are friends. She is my "best buddy." And if you are married and you do not like your spouse, find the redeeming qualities in his or her life and learn to like them.

2. To stay married, look for commonality of culture.

When I say to marry within your culture, I am not talking about black culture, white culture, Hispanic culture, or oriental culture. I am talking about the culture of your true race: Christian. Marry within your culture. Paul wrote in 2 Corinthians 6:14:

> **Be not unequally yoked together with unbelievers: for what fellowship hath righteousness with unrighteousness? and what communion hath light with darkness?**

If you are a believer looking for a spouse, do not look in bars or other places where you will find unbelievers. Look within your culture for a spouse.

If you are a Christian married to an unbeliever, put everything you can into your marriage so that your husband or wife will want to become born again. Then your marriage will be based on a commonality of culture. Even if your spouse never makes that commitment to Christ, at least when you stand before the judgment seat of God, your conscience will be clear. (1 Cor. 7:13,14,17.)

If an unbelieving husband or wife departs, according to the Word of God, you are free to marry whomever you choose, as long as the one you marry is in the faith. (1 Cor. 7:15.)

That principle deals with the foundation of a marriage, the spiritual, most important part. However, as a common sense guideline, not as a scriptural principle, it also helps with compatibility in the natural for both partners to be from a similar culture. If you are a "redneck bubba," more than likely marriage to an "uptown," sophisticated woman will not work out.

You may come in all excited one day and say, "Let's go fishing. I have a can of worms."

More than likely, she will say, "I don't do worms."

Marry someone with whom you have some culture commonality. If you are already married and have no cultural commonality, you need to find some things of natural interest with which to shore up your relationship.

3. Get your parents in agreement.

If you are going to get married, try to marry someone whom your parents like — or plan on living a long distance away from them! Do your best to get your parents in agreement.

4. Marry, and stay married, with finances in mind.

I certainly do not mean to marry or stay married for money. However, considering finances is very important before getting married and certainly a good thing to do before you decide to break up! When people get divorced, they usually both end up broke. I have never seen it fail. Do you want financial hardship? Get divorced. You have alimony, child support, and all kinds of aggravations.

You cannot live on love. Ecclesiastes 10:19 says that "money answers all things." People who say two can live as cheaply as one are lying, because today two people cannot live as cheaply as one. The number one cause of arguments in most marriages is money, or specifically, the lack of money.

If you are looking for a husband or wife, the first thing is to make sure that person you like is a Christian. The second thing is to make certain that he or she has a job. Understand the importance of prosperity. God wants you to prosper. God will help you to prosper. You do not want to be poor.

Marry with money in mind. Marry with some idea of where you want to live on the social/economic ladder. And husbands and wives, you need to be in agreement about your financial lifestyle. Everyone does not want to live the "lifestyle of the rich and famous."

If your goal in life is to live a comfortable, middle-class lifestyle, that ought to be a point of agreement.

If your idea of a perfect lifestyle is living back in the woods with the wild animals, and your spouse is in agreement, build a cabin and have a good time.

The important thing is that you understand money matters in marriage.

5. Marry or stay married for political or social advantage.

Do you know why the rich or politically active usually stay married? They marry for political and social advantage. The Bible is full of examples, in addition to the story of Rebekah and Isaac.

In the book of Esther, we see that a man named Mordecai entered his beautiful young cousin, Esther, in a "royal beauty contest," and she became the queen of Persia. (Esth. 2:1-17.) Later, her people, the Jews, became in danger of being exterminated because a royal official was trying to destroy Mordecai. (Esth. 3:1-6.)

Mordecai, a gatekeeper at the palace, told his cousin, "Perhaps you were born into Persia at this time and place to save your people." (Esth. 4:14.)

Esther married for political and social advantage. Personally, I like the concept of founding a dynasty and of families joining together who can help one another. It is a biblical concept. It is one that most of us today do not think of, because we believe we are supposed to marry for love.

However, if you have married because God is "building your dynasty," or for natural, social and political advantage, when rough times come, it is easier to stay married. There are things to cement you together besides love. In spite of the present "folk knowledge" that love conquers all, and "the world well lost" for love, it is not true. Love, as the world counts love, will not last through hard times.

We counsel many people who married because they were "in love," and now they want to kill each other. Some of you readers know what I am talking about. Obviously, love is not the ultimate reason to get married. I love my wife, and she loves me, but we have a wonderful marriage because there are plenty of *other* reasons to stay married.

6. Marry someone who will go the second mile.

Rebekah did not just give the unnamed servant a drink of water. She drew enough water for his ten camels. Camels are some of the ugliest creatures God ever created. Not only are they ugly, but they also have a horrible stench. Not only do they have a horrible stench, but they have cantankerous dispositions. A camel will try to bite you while you are giving it water or feed, even if it is dying of hunger or thirst.

Yet, this beautiful girl not only gave water to a man she does not know, but also drew water for his ten ugly, smelly, cantankerous camels. That is the kind of woman I married, someone willing to go the second mile.

Jesus said that if someone compelled you to go a mile, to go with him two. (Matt. 5:41.)

I love 1 Peter 3:8,9:

> **Finally, be ye all of one mind, having compassion one of another, love as brethren, be pitiful, be courteous:**

> **Not rendering evil for evil, or railing for railing: but contrariwise blessing; knowing that ye are thereunto called, that ye should inherit a blessing.**

Why is it so many husbands and wives can be nice to everyone except the one to whom they are married?

Do you want to know how to avoid arguments in your marriage? Do not argue. You may say you argue because your spouse is argumentative. However, you can solve that. When your spouse argues, do not respond with counter arguments. Give a soft answer (Prov. 15:1), and do not be pulled into the other person's "storm." Be nice, be kind, be courteous, and your marriage will be blessed with peace.

7. Get married and stay married because that is God's plan.

If you are a Christian and unmarried, do not get married until you know it is God's plan for you. There are some things we want at times that are not in His plan for us yet. Find the plan of God.

Proverbs 16:9 says:

> A man's heart deviseth his way: but the Lord directeth his steps.

The Lord directed the steps of Abraham's servant. The Lord directed Rebekah's steps. If you want to know the plan of God for your life, how to find it is just as simple as Romans 12:1,2:

> I beseech you therefore, brethren, by the mercies of God, that ye present your bodies a living sacrifice, holy, acceptable unto God, which is your reasonable service.
>
> And be not conformed to this world: but be ye transformed by the renewing of your mind, that ye may prove what is that good, and acceptable, and perfect, will of God.

Put your wants and desires to one side, and let God's plan be fulfilled in your life. Husbands and wives, if you want to stay married:

*Submit yourselves to God.

*Present your bodies a living sacrifice, holy and acceptable unto God.

*Make a mutual covenant, a commitment that together you are going to seek the plan of God, know the plan of God, and fulfill the plan of God for your lives.

If you will do these things, you will have a blessed home and a blessed marriage.

8. Get some help from that unnamed "servant."

Isaac is a type of Christ. Rebekah is a type of the Church. In the New Testament, Jesus is equated with a bridegroom and the Church with a bride. The unnamed servant of Abraham is a type of the Holy Spirit Who brings you into a personal relationship with Christ.

You become part of the Bride of Christ when you are born again. Get help from that "Unnamed Servant."

If you are single and want a husband or wife, you need to pray, "Holy Spirit, help me. I haven't been doing too well on my own."

Then, submit yourself to God as you are led by the Spirit of God. He will help you find the right person. The Holy Spirit helped us. I started dating when I was saved at 15 years of age. At that time, in our church, teenagers thought they had to be "going steady" with someone.

In our youth group, we seemed to change "steady" couples every five or six weeks. Each time, I just knew this was the one. About five weeks later, I would be tired of my girlfriend, and we would break up. Some nice Christian folks tried very hard to fix me up with girls. Let me give you a word of wisdom — do not let good Christian folk "fix you up" with dates. They will mess you up, not fix you up.

Finally, I did what I am advising you to do. I started praying, and I prayed diligently. One day not long after that, Connie walked into the church. God had to send her from a denominational church into my Pentecostal church.

I asked her if she wanted to sit by me, and she asked her mother. Her mother said yes, but after the service, her mother went to the Pastor and asked about me, which was the right thing to do. Our pastor indicated his approval.

When Connie and I went on our first date, we walked down to the local convenience store. I only had a quarter, so I could only buy one soft drink. I took a few sips, then she took a few sips. That was our first date.

Our second date was even more exciting. We went to the New Year's Eve watch-night service at the church, and afterwards, my best friend took us out for pizza. (I still had no money.) After that, we just grew up together in church.

The Holy Spirit knows just what He's doing. Get help from that unnamed servant.

9. Look for the comfort factor.

Isaac was out meditating in the field. By the way, ladies, as I wrote earlier, if you are not married and want to be married, find a man who prays. Isaac was out praying in the evening. And, men, if you are not married and you want to be married, pray.

Isaac was praying when he saw the unnamed servant coming back with his bride-to-be. Rebekah jumped off her camel and went to meet him, and he was comforted by her. Always look for the comfort factor.

Ecclesiastes 4:11 says that if two people lie together, they have heat, but one cannot have heat alone. That scripture has nothing to do with sex. It has to do with comfort.

Have you noticed that up to this point, none of the reasons for getting married is sex. You want to know why? That is because sex is not nearly as important as most folk think it is. If you marry for lust, you will be in worse trouble then if you just marry for romantic love.

Conversely, if you have all of the rest of these concepts working in your marriage, sex will generally take care of itself.

Connie and I have married friends who talk about what they would do if their husbands or wives died. Some of them sat around our table one night discussing this. The conversation was alien to me, because I am praying preservation on my wife because she is comfortable. That may not sound very romantic to you, but I really like the comfort level.

"Comfort" also means knowing what someone is going to do. I am predictable in my unpredictability. My wife and I have a comfort level, which means that if I say something that would offend 98 percent of the rest of the women in the world, it will not offend her. We are comfortable with one another. If she says something that would offend most men, we hang together. We are comfortable in our relationship.

When you find the comfort factor, you can stay together just because it works.

10. Isaac loved Rebekah.

The very last principle you will find in the story of Isaac and Rebekah is that, if the other nine are in place, you will love one another. The best definition of love is 1 Corinthians 13:4. If you translated charity from Elizabethan English to modern English, that verse would read this way:

> Love is longsuffering and kind; love does
> not envy; love does not get into pride and con-

sider one's own "rights"; love does not want its own way and is not easily provoked; love thinks no evil of another and rejoices in truth, not iniquity; love reveals all things, believes all things, hopes all things, and endures all things. Love never fails.

If you have that kind of mutual love in your marriage, you will have a happy marriage. If you go into a marriage with that kind of love, you will always stay together.

Endnotes

[1] *Strong's*, "Greek Dictionary," p. 75, #5293.

[2] *Ibid.*, p. 54, #3860.

[3] *Ibid.*, "Hebrew and Chaldee Dictionary," p. 51, #3227, and p. 107, #7259.

12

Children, Challenges, and Changes

Whenever I write or preach concerning the family or home life, I run the danger of someone trying to apply the things that work in my circumstances to their circumstances, which will not always work. Biblical principles will work in any case, but they must be applied differently in different circumstances. So, I need to set the scenario before you read any further.

As I said in the last chapter, my wife and I have been happily married for more than twenty-two years. We have three children, two teenagers and a twenty-year-old. Our oldest has moved out on her own and is sharing an apartment with two other young ladies.

Connie and I have gone through all of the interesting things of rearing children. We have one child successfully through the teenage years, and the other two are coming right along. They have been into the usual scrapes kids get themselves into, but they are good kids. That is my perspective for sharing what I am about to share with you.

Every family is not a traditional nuclear family. Oftentimes it is "his, hers, and ours." Some of you know what I am talking about. You have a different scenario. You have to apply the Word of God as it fits your situation.

Psalm 127:3 says that children are our heritage from the Lord and the fruit of the womb is our reward. Children are our heritage from the Lord; however, children are creatures of chaos. You have probably noticed that children are chaotic by nature.

I do not know what your marital relationship was like before your children came into the world, but my wife and I were having a wonderful time. We were pastoring in northern Oklahoma when we decided we wanted children. In the due process of time, a beautiful baby girl was born to us. Our lives have not been the same since!

Up to that point, we could pack up and get on the road in a few minutes. After the birth of our first child, it was: Do you have the diapers? Do you have the formula? Is the baby bag packed? Do you have the baby bed packed? Where are the baby's toys? Then about the time we got to church, the baby would vomit on one of us.

I hope you will not misunderstand my "tongue-in-cheek" observations. We would not go back to being without children or trade ours for anything in the world. However, there is no denying the fact that in the natural order of things, children are creatures of chaos.

Children will continue in chaos unless they are checked, unless their lives are molded and shaped by their parents. The tragedy to a child being allowed to live in unchecked chaos is that chaos kills. The first commandment given man with a promise is to honor your parents *so that your life may be prolonged on earth.* (Eph. 6:2,3.)

Do you know that 95 percent of all of the teenage murders and of all the teenagers who murder teenagers in the entire world take place in one nation — the United States of America? Chaos kills kids.

There are parents who will not parent. Some children divorce their parents, refusing to acknowledge that their parents have any rights or responsibilities over their lives. There is chaos in our social system concerning parents and children. There is no real security in our "social" system.

Millions of people have paid into Social Security since it was enacted in the thirties. I hope the fund is still there when I retire. However, that seems an impossibility because there are too many of us "Baby Boomers." By the time I retire, there will be three people drawing out of the system for every one still paying into it. So I am not trusting in Social Security.

Let me tell you what real "social security" is:

It is having a godly family structure.

It is rearing your children according to biblical principles so that you have a family unit that is intact and built on the Word of God.

Chaotic conditions demand that you recognize your responsibilities. As parents, you have a responsibility toward your children, and children have a responsibility toward their parents. Ephesians 6:1-3 states:

> **Children, obey your parents in the Lord: for this is right.**
>
> **Honour thy father and mother; which is the first commandment with promise;**
>
> **That it may be well with thee, and thou mayest live long on the earth.**

Children's Rights

Do you know why you have responsibility to train and teach your children? It is so that your children can live long on the earth and be blessed of God. Parents, you are responsible for training and nurturing your children; and children, you are responsible to be in obedience to your parents. (Col. 3:20.)

Some children may ask, "Well, what about children's rights?"

Children's rights according to the Word of God are to honor their fathers and their mothers. Of course, children do have certain "rights":

Children have a right to food.

Children have a right to clothing.

Children have a right to freedom from abuse.

Children have a right to be taught.

Children have a right to be loved.

After that, everything else is a privilege. Rights bring responsibilities and, if children have not yet assumed the responsibilities, their rights are rather limited. The person who pays the bills has the authority and power.

That is why the welfare system is so devastating to a family because a child realizes that mom and dad are not paying the bills. The state is paying the bills, and the one who has the responsibility has the rights.

A family is not a democracy. It is a benevolent dictatorship. Ephesians 6:4 tells us the father's responsibility:

> **And, ye fathers, provoke not your children to wrath: but bring them up in the nurture and admonition of the Lord.**

God called fathers to be the spiritual leaders of the house. Men, take your positions and assume the responsibilities of spiritual leaders of your homes.

Not "provoking your children to wrath" does not mean to let them have their own way all of the time or they will get mad at you. That is permissiveness, not love, and not fulfilling your responsibility.

Do you know what provokes children to wrath? Here are some of the things that will:

*A double standard, or inconsistency in your own life, will provoke a child to wrath.

*Not meaning what you say, saying one thing and doing another, will provoke your children.

*Unfair discipline will provoke your children to wrath, such as favoring one child over another or punishing them much too hard for minor offenses.

*Being too busy to spend quality time with your children that affirms their worth to you will build rejection into their personalities. Sooner or later, that will result in a core of anger in them that affects themselves and lashes out at others.

Nurture is used one time in the Bible. (Eph. 6:4.) The Greek word *paideia* means "tutorage as in education or training," and "by implication, disciplinary correction."[1] In other words, proper "nurturing" includes proper disciple and correction.

If you discipline and correct your children, society will not have to. Somewhere along the line, your children are going to learn discipline and correction, even if it is jail or the penitentiary.

In Proverbs, where King Solomon, the wisest man of his time, wrote a collection of wisdom sayings on many subjects, the Bible talks about "the rod" of discipline. There is more than one Hebrew word for *rod*, but *shebet* is used in the verses about children.

Literally, it means "a stick (for punishing, writing, fighting, ruling, walking, etc.)." In the context of disciplining children, it obviously means a "hickory," as it is called in the South, or some implement that is not hard enough to hurt a child, but one that will get his or her attention.

When our children became old enough to need such discipline, we got an old leather belt and doubled it up so that it would make an impact but not hurt very badly. According to child psychologists and child workers, doubling a belt makes it pop so that it sounds a lot worse than it is. We would give our children one swat and about a ten-minute talk. They would rather have had the swat than the talk, but it worked.

There are several proverbs about "the rod" of discipline:

> He that spareth his rod hateth his son: but he that loveth him chasteneth him betimes.
>
> Proverbs 13:24

> Foolishness is bound in the heart of a child; but the rod of correction shall drive it far from him.
>
> Proverbs 22:15

> Withhold not correction from the child: for if thou beatest him with the rod, he shall not die.
>
> Thou shalt beat him with the rod, and shalt deliver his soul from hell.
>
> Proverbs 23:13,14

> The rod and reproof give wisdom: but a child left to himself bringeth his mother to shame.
>
> Proverbs 29:15

My wife and I were in a restaurant the other day, and we were blessed at seeing the way a young couple handled their child, who needed discipline in public. The little boy was being rowdy and running through the restaurant.

I was sitting there thinking our meal was about to be spoiled, when the father turned and looked at the little boy, and said, "That's one."

I thought to myself, "Right on, dad!"

When our children were growing up, Connie and I decided that we were not going to have the kind of family that is always in chaos with parents screaming at the children and at each other. We decided we would have an orderly home life so that when our children came to an age where they became accountable for their own actions, they would know discipline. We used the same system as the father in the restaurant.

When our children misbehaved, we would say, "That's one." They knew that was an indication their behavior was not acceptable. If they continued to misbehave, we would say, "That's two." Two meant they had better stop whatever they were doing immediately under penalty of a number three. And if perchance they did not heed the parental warning of one or two, they got a "three."

If they got a "three," they knew that, at our convenience, not theirs, they would be taken to one side, reproved, and swatted with the belt I described above. Accompanying the swat would be a talk on why what they had been doing was wrong and what they should have been doing. The swat got their attention, the talk brought correction.

Because we brought order into their chaos at home, we did not have to worry about our children acting up while we were sitting on the platform during a service. Once in a while, when they were very young, they would "try" us. They knew we would not get off of the platform to correct them, so many times they would continue to do whatever they were doing.

However, when they got that "two," everything stopped. One time I can remember, John, our son, did not even heed the "two." I gave him a "three," and knowing he was in big trouble, he crawled under the front seat. But that did not change anything. He had kept on until he merited a "three," and "threes" were irrevocable.

There was no grace from a three. There was grace in two. There was goodness in one. But, once they had a three, they were in deep, deep trouble. God called parents "to nurture, to bring up, to discipline, and to correct."

However, I have noticed that many parents, especially Spirit-filled parents, "major on minors" instead of being reasonable. If your teenager is fifteen or sixteen and has to be in bed at 9:30 p.m., he or she is going to rebel, I promise you! Major on major issues, and let the minor ones slide by.

Parents, your ultimate goal ought to be to instill godly values into the hearts and lives of your children. That is where the word *admonition* comes in. (Eph. 6:4.) It means "calling attention to, i.e., (by implication) mild rebuke or warning."[3]

God gave Israel the best way to rear children in Deuteronomy 6:6,7:

> **And these words, which I command thee this day, shall be in thine heart:**
>
> **And thou shalt teach them diligently unto thy children, and shalt talk of them when thou sittest in**

> thine house, and when thou walkest by the way, and when thou liest down, and when thou risest up.

In Deuteronomy 32:46,47 Moses reiterated God's instructions about teaching the children of the Israelites His Word:

> And he said unto them, Set your hearts unto all the words which I testify among you this day, which ye shall command your children to observe to do, all the words of this law.
>
> For it is not a vain thing for you; because it is your life: and through this thing ye shall prolong your days in the land, whither ye go over Jordan to possess it.

Teach your children the Word of God and how to live by it.

Train your children to be Christians. And, as Christians, there are three things you need to teach your children and three things you ought to know. First of all, you should know that you cannot teach anything that you have not experienced.

Three Things To Teach Children

1. You need to teach your children *propitiation*.

What is *propitiation*, you may ask? It means "to be merciful" or "to make reconciliation for."[4] It means that Jesus died on the cross as an eternal sin offering to make reconciliation with the Father for mankind.

In Exodus 12:26, the Israelites were celebrating the passover for the first time. They killed a lamb, took its blood, and put it on the door post and up over the top of the door. And the death angel passed over Israel because they were covered by the blood. That is *propitiation*.

> And it shall come to pass, when your children shall say unto you, What mean ye by this service?
>
> That ye shall say, It is a sacrifice of the Lord's passover, who passed over the houses of the children of Israel in Egypt, when he smote the Egyptians, and delivered our houses. And the people bowed the head and worshipped.
>
> Exodus 12:26,27

You need to teach your children that Jesus saves, and that His blood is sufficient to cover the most vile of sins. They need to know that they can have redemption through His blood, according to Ephesians 1:7. Redemption is a reality that means they have been delivered from the powers of darkness and translated into the Kingdom of God's dear Son. (Col. 1:13,14.)

Tell your child, "He was buried in the tomb for you. He was resurrected on the third day for you. He is standing at the right hand of the Father interceding for you, and He has become your eternal sin offering."

> And he is the propitiation for our sins: and not for ours only, but also for the sins of the whole world.
>
> In this was manifested the love of God toward us, because that God sent his only begotten Son into the world, that we might live through him.
>
> 1 John 2:2, 4:9

You need to teach your children that there is no other name under heaven given among men whereby they can be saved except the name of Jesus. (Acts 4:12.)

2. The second thing God told Israel to teach their children is *sanctification.* It follows propitiation. Teach your children that Jesus not only saves them from their sins but also sanctifies them and sets them apart from sin. Paul wrote in 1 Corinthians 1:30 that we are in Christ

Jesus, Who has been made unto us "wisdom, righteousness, sanctification, and redemption."

It is not enough to be saved, you have to stay saved, which means you have to *live* saved. Many people are living under "greasy grace," which means a person lives any way he or she wants to, and still calls on the name of the Lord. God loves unconditionally. His grace is beyond comprehension. But because of His love and grace, He corrects and sanctifies our lives just as we correct our children.

God is not unconditionally permissive. Simply because He loves us unconditionally, He will chastise us for our good. Otherwise, He would not be a good Father. Read John 17:23 and John 14:23. He loves you enough to correct you, to let you know you are wrong. He moves by His Spirit to make everything in our lives "right."

Having been set apart by the word of Jesus, having been sanctified by His blood, how are you continually sanctified? How does God makes things "right"?

John 17:17 says we are sanctified through the truth, which is God's Word. Just as God teaches us from His Word, teach your children the Word of God. Teach them right from wrong based on biblical principles and precepts.

While you are teaching them right from wrong, get them in church. When people bring their children to church, they are saying to their children that the house of God and the Word of God have value in their lives. Keep your children in church.

I was reading an interview with Alice Cooper, a famous "shock rocker" of the seventies, a weird entertainer who bit the head off of a bat and had to get rabies shots. He told the interviewer that he and his family attended First Presbyterian Church in Chicago. Every Sunday morning he and his wife took their four-year-old daughter to Sunday school.

He said it was important that children are not sent to church but are *taken* to church. If Alice Cooper has enough sense to understand that, why not the rest of us?

When I was growing up, I was no different than all children still operating in chaos. The only time I prayed was Sunday morning.

I would wake up on Sunday morning and say, "Oh, Lord, don't let us go to church today."

I did not want to go to church. I went anyway. Today, we have a rule at our house: If you live under our roof, you go to church. It has never been an option for our children.

A lady told me once, "If I make my children go to church, they're going to grow up hating church."

I responded, "No, if you don't make your children go to church, they'll grow up as heathens."

Most of you reading this book probably also were brought up in church and may have hated having to go. As soon as you were old enough, you may have quit going to church — until you fell on your face often enough.

Then came the time when you woke up in the pig pen like the son who had been so prodigal with his inheritance (Luke 15) and said, "I think I'll go back to church."

The "prodigal" son said, "I think I'll go back to my father's house."

He returned home to find his father with his arms outstretched, full of forgiveness.

If you can relate to the prodigal's experience, and God saved you, changed you, and turned your life around, I am sure you have been in the house of God ever since. Perhaps you now have children in church.

And your children are saying, "I don't like going to church."

You need to be saying, "I'm training you up in the way you should go and when you're old, you will not depart from it." (Prov. 22:6.)

3. The third thing God told Israel to teach their children was *appropriation*. Teach them to appropriate all of God's promises, from salvation to blessings. (Rom. 10:9,10; Gal. 3:6-9.) Second Corinthians 1:20 says:

> **For all the promises of God in him are yea, and in him Amen, unto the glory of God by us.**

Teach your children that your God is a God Who answers prayer.

Teach your children that your God is a God Who honors faith.

Teach your children to be "faith walkers." Hebrews 11:1 says:

> **Now faith is the substance of things hoped for, the evidence of things not seen.**

Hebrew 11:6 says:

> **But without faith it is impossible to please him; for he that cometh to God must believe that he is, and that he is a rewarder of them that diligently seek him.**

In Matthew 9:29, Jesus told two blind men, **according to your faith be it unto you,** and to the man with the possessed son, Jesus said, **If thou canst believe, all**

things are possible to him that believeth (Mark 9:23).

Teach your children to believe God in order that they may become boys and girls of faith, and then men and women of faith.

Knowledge Brings Opportunities

Do you realize the opportunity that you have as a parent who understands the Word of God?

How much junk did you have to unlearn to get where you are?

How much tradition did you have to plow through or lay to one side to get to the place in God that you are now?

Do you realize the opportunity you have as a parent to teach your child principles from God's Word and to teach them faith instead of unbelief so they do not have to wade through the chaos you did?

Can you imagine what your children can be like if you teach them principles of faith and not of unbelief?

It will bring them to a place where they can reach out and lay hold of and claim the promises of God. Teach your children appropriation. Teach them how to believe. Teach them to expect when they pray. Teach them how to claim the promise of God, and then Psalm 115:14 will become a reality in their lives. The Lord will increase you more and more. God wants you to increase, and God wants your children to increase.

While you are teaching your children appropriation, teach them how to tithe. We have taught our children to be tithers. Just as with most of the other things, we teach our children to bring order into their lives. In the beginning they did not like it. However,

God did not say to teach your children what they like, but what they need in order to have their steps ordered of Him.

Our daughter who, as the oldest, was the first to begin to get her own money would get $10, and I would ask, "Baby, did you pay your tithes?"

At first, I got all sorts of answers. I remember one time she said, "I'm not supposed to tithe. I'm a kid."

I said, "Time out! I rebuke that thought."

Then she said, "Why to I have to tithe? I'm the pastor's daughter."

I explained that, first of all, tithes do not go to the pastor. They go to support the Lord's work in the church in general. Secondly, she was to tithe because I did not want any cursed children under my roof.

So we taught our children to tithe, and they have tithed. Even at these late teenage and early adult stages in their lives, occasionally I will ask them if they have paid their tithes. And they will say, "Yes, Dad." I want my children to be blessed. I want them to grow up knowing Jehovah Jireh, the Lord Who provides.

Let me show you from their experience the "flip side" of tithing, the incoming as well as the outgoing. There has never been a time when any of our children wanted to work that they did not have a job. One went into the burger- flipping business. They have never had a time when they needed a job that a job was not there, because, early on, they came to understand the principles of tithing, sowing, and reaping.

Teach your children appropriation. Teach them how to lay hold of the promises and blessings of God. Teach your children and teach them well.

Proverbs 22:6 tells us that if we train up a child in the way he ought to go, God's way, when he is old he will not depart from that training. That verse means, according to one translator, "to touch the palate" of your child.

In other words, touch their tastes. For example, both my wife and I like asparagus. When it is in season, we eat asparagus.

Do children like asparagus? No.

Do they eat asparagus? Yes, they do at our house, because we are the parents who are in charge. If Connie cooks it, the children eat it, even if they do not like it.

I did not like asparagus when I was growing up. In fact, I hated it. I tried not to eat it, but I grew up under the same kind of order that we have in our own home. If my mother cooked it, we ate it! Then, one day when I was an adult, all of a sudden it hit me that I wanted some asparagus. I have been voluntarily eating asparagus ever since. My palate was touched by the taste when I was young.

Some reader might be wondering what asparagus has to do with the Kingdom of God. The point is that, however you "touch the palate of your child," or whatever taste you put in your child, when he is old, he will go back to that "taste."

Touch his spirit when he is young and teach him the Word of God, and when he is old, he will not depart from his taste for God.

My primary concern as a Christian parent is that I want my children to go to heaven. There are only two places to go. There is only one alternative to heaven, and I do not want my children to go there. Also, I want my children to be everything God has called them to be. That is my responsibility and my wife's responsibility.

I will close this chapter by encouraging all parents with one thought: If you have trained your children up in the way they should go, you have a security, in more ways than one. The Bible says they *will not* depart from that. First Timothy 5:4 says:

> But if any widow have children or nephews, let them learn first to show piety at home, and to requite their parents: for that is good and acceptable before God.

What does that mean? It means that if the time comes when you are old and cannot take care of yourself, you have someone who will take care of you. That is God's "Social Security program."

Bless your children every day. For those of you who are struggling, there is help. Jesus will help you. Put the Word of God in those children's lives. There are outside influences trying to destroy your children, but pray preservation on their lives and God will honor you.

If you are a single parent and a Christian, you are not parenting by yourself. You have One with you "sticking closer than a brother" (Prov. 18:24), Who sees everything you are going through and is more than ready to help if you call on Him. If you do not have what people would call a "picture-perfect" family, keep serving the Lord, and He will change your family for good.

You may be reading this book and thinking, "I'm not a Christian, but I would like to be. I would like to have a Christian family. I have read this chapter, and it all makes a lot of sense. I would like God's help in my life and in my family.

"I want to know Jesus as my Savior. I want to know that He has set me apart. I want to know that I can claim the promises of God because of what Jesus has done. I want to know that I am on my way to heaven and be able to teach my children how to go to heaven."

In short, if you are reading this book and you need to be saved . . . or perhaps you are a backslider, one who has fallen away from God, but in your heart you know it is time to come back to the Father's house . . . or if you have been a "lukewarm" Christian who needs to rededicate and recommit your life to Christ, then lift your hand to heaven and pray this prayer out loud:

> *Father God, forgive me of my sins, my short-comings, and my failures. Change me; transform me. Make me a new creature in Christ. Let the joy of the Lord be my strength and the power of God be my shield. I believe in my heart what I confess with my mouth and that is that Jesus is my Savior and He is my Lord. I believe it is done, in Jesus' name.*

Endnotes

[1] *Strong's*, "Greek Dictionary," p. 54, #3809.
[2] *Ibid.*, "Hebrew and Chaldee Dictionary," P. 111, #7626.
[3] *Ibid.*, "Greek Dictionary," p. 50, #3559.
[4] *Ibid.*, p. 37, #2434, 2435.

13

Ordering Your Life for Supernatural Living

In John 6, we read the story of Jesus feeding five thousand men with two fishes and five loaves. Those men, when they had seen the miracle that Jesus did, said, "This is truly the prophet of whom it was prophesied." (John 6:14.)

Of course, if you read the rest of the chapter, you will find the very same men were the ones who forsook Him when Jesus said of Himself, "I am the bread of life." (John 6:48,51.)

Out of that story of the five fishes and two loaves, I want to show you seven keys to *super* natural living, not seven keys to the supernatural.

I have discovered that God working a miracle in an individual's life does not insure that person's stability in faith. In fact, oftentimes, those who have seen the greatest miracles have the most instability. This is a generation where people want to touch the spectacular supernatural, just as in Jesus' day when the Pharisees were always wanting a "sign." (Matt. 12:39.)

There is something better than touching the supernatural, because there are certain situations that could have a different solution, more in line with God's order. God wants all of His children to move into the place of *super* natural living.

Take a moment and think about why those men needed a miracle. Why does anyone need a miracle? If you need a miracle, it is indicative that you are in a crisis situation.

When you prayed, "Lord, give me a miracle," why did you need a miracle? You were in a mess. Would it not be better to live above the mess so that you did not need a miracle?

Some Christians are so heavenly minded, they are no earthly good. At the other extreme, some are so earthly minded, they are no heavenly good. Between the two extremes is a nice place of balance. God loves to prove Himself. God loves to take your natural, touch it, and use it to meet the needs of your life. That is true *super* natural living.

It is getting a promotion when no one else is getting promoted.

It is getting a job when no one else is being hired.

God giving you favor is *super* natural living. God putting you at the right place at the right time, causing people to come across your path that normally would not cross your path is living a *super* natural life. You may be looking for an angel from heaven, when God wants to send you an "angel" from earth.

It is the nature of the Father to nurture and to meet needs. Let's look at the seven keys to supernatural living in the natural, which are found in the story of loaves and fishes.

Seven Keys to Supernatural Living

1. God is not limited by lack.

David wrote about his forefathers in Psalm 78:19,20:

> Yea, they spake against God; they said, Can God furnish a table in the wilderness?

> Behold, he smote the rock, that the waters gushed out, and the streams overflowed; can he give bread also? can he provide flesh for his people?

They said that even after God had shown Himself in their travels in miracles, signs, and wonders. Yet, whenever there was a lack, either real or perceived, they were quick to sneer, doubt, and question God's power and goodness.

God was very "wroth" with them, David wrote in remembrance. He said that, for all they saw of God's goodness and grace, they still sinned and did not believe His wonderful works. (Ps. 78:32.)

They did not understand that God has no lack and that He wants to meet the needs of His people. In fact, if there is lack in your life, then you just have an opportunity for God to provide abundantly. Jesus said He came to earth, lived, and died that we might have life more abundantly. (John 10:10.)

The Israelites asked sarcastically if God could furnish a table in the wilderness. They said, "Can God," and God said, "I can!" God did furnish food and water in the wilderness, and He can furnish a table in the wilderness of your life. You are serving a God well able to meet your needs, because there is no lack in the Kingdom of God. Romans 4:17 describes the very nature of God:

> . . . Even God who quickeneth the dead, and calleth those things which be not as though they were.

Because of His nature, when God speaks a thing it comes into existence. There is no lack in God.

In testifying of Himself in Psalm 50:12, God said, "If I were hungry, I would not tell you, because the world is mine and everything in it."

God is not limited by your lack.

2. Use what you have.

Jesus required "loaves and fishes" for a miracle. He always requires that we use what we have. Another biblical example of this principle is found in 2 Kings 4:1-7.

A widow of a prophet came to Elisha saying, "My husband was one of your servants. He was one of the sons of the prophets. Now he is dead, and our creditors are taking my sons to sell to pay the bills we owe. What are we going do?"

Elisha said, "Tell me what you have in the house."

She told the prophet all she had was a pot of oil. Then he told her to *use what she had*. In addition, she was to add to what she had by borrowing all of the vessels (jars, bottles, pots) that she could from the neighbors. After she had brought all of those into the house, she was to shut the door and start pouring out of that little pot of oil. As long as she had vessels to fill, oil flowed out of the pot.

She used what she had, and God met her lack. This was a supernaturally manifested miracle based on what she already had, just as the miracle of the loaves and fishes was based on what they had on hand. You have to use what you have, and then you will find that what you have is enough.

You may say, "But you don't know my inadequacies. You do not know my inabilities."

No, but I know what the Word of God said about an inadequate member of the tribe of Manasseh named Gideon. I know how God used Gideon.

I also know Gideon's response to the call of God in Judges 6:15: "My family is the poorest in Manasseh, and I am the least in my family."

His family had never done well, so Gideon believed he would never do well. Yet, when the hand of God came on him, Gideon led the Israelites out from under Midianite oppression. When God touches the natural life of any man or woman, that life becomes a supernatural life and they are used of God. You must use what you have.

3. Set yourself in order.

It may be prudent to reiterate that there are some people who cannot be helped. That is not a judgment; that is an observation. Some people's lives are like a sieve. You can pour water into a sieve, and it will flow right out. Instead if a solid bottom to the vessel, there is a net. A sieve is designed to "sift." God did not design your life to be sifted. God designed you as a vessel to be filled.

The first miracle that Jesus did involved six waterpots made out of stone. The hosts at a wedding reception needed more wine. Jesus' mother told the servants to do whatever He told them to do. As the servants obeyed Jesus' command to fill the waterpots to the brim with water, the water turned into the very best wine. (John 2:1-11.)

Notice, however, that Jesus used what He had in the natural to supernaturally meet a need. There were waterpots to *be* filled. His first miracle speaks of the new birth, of the transformation wrought in the life of someone who comes to know Jesus.

The waterpots never changed on the exterior. They were transformed on the interior. They were natural vessels filled with the supernatural goodness of God. You were made a vessel to be filled with the goodness of God. The pots were in order, and the servants operated in order by obeying Jesus' commands.

There has to be order if you are going to live a supernatural lifestyle. In 1 Corinthians 12:18, Paul wrote that God set the members in the Body as it pleased Him. That means you have a place in the Church. You need to find your place and sit down in it.

The first thing Jesus did in the incident of the loaves and fishes was to command the men to sit down in companies. Luke wrote that they were ordered in companies of fifty. (Luke 9:14), and Mark wrote that the people sat down by "ranks" of hundreds and fifties. (Mark 6:39,40.)

The point is that, before the supernatural miracle could be manifested and the loaves and fishes multiplied, everyone had to sit down in order. So it is not enough to sit down with whatever you have and wait on the Lord. You must sit down in order.

Ephesians 2:6 tells us that we are not only raised up together but made to sit *together* in heavenly places in Christ Jesus. It is interesting that the word *together* is used twice. We are raised up together, and we are made to sit together. The Body of Christ will only function properly as we recognize those two facts.

For God to touch your natural life supernaturally and for you to live that supernatural lifestyle, you have to recognize that all have been raised up together. Sitting together is an attitude of rest. You are not struggling. You are not striving.

You have found your place, and you are sitting at rest in your place knowing you are unique in the Body of Christ. You are unique in the Church. No one can take your place.

Because I have always delegated a lot of authority to my staff, people used to ask me if I were not afraid someone would split the church. My response has always been that if someone can take my place, he probably should. I have built churches, and I could probably build another one. But, you see, I know no one can take my place in the church where God set me.

That is a wonderful place to be, knowing you are where God wants you to be and that no one can take your place. You do not have to worry about someone coming up behind you, moving you out of the way, and taking your place.

The most frustrated people in any church are those who have never found their place or who are trying to take a place God did not intend for them. Every church has at least one frustrated singer who cannot sing, but who wants to be the church diva.

Find your place, and whatever place that is, enjoy your place in God. If you are fulfilling your calling to the Body of Christ, if you are fulfilling your responsibility in God, when you stand before the judgment seat of Christ, you are going to be rewarded equally with everyone else who has fulfilled his or her place and position.

I love Dr. Billy Graham. He does not preach red-hot, Holy-Ghost, miracle-deliverance, devil-chasing sermons. He does not even usually raise his voice as he preaches salvation. Yet, he has done a work for the Body of Christ and has ministered to the world. I admire and respect him. He has stood the test of time.

I am encouraged by what I know about God's Word and His ways, because I know that, although I have not done what Billy Graham has done, when I get to heaven I am going to get the same reward. We are rewarded for obedience and faithfulness to the work God has called us to do, not for the size of the work we have done.

The man I mentioned earlier who opens and closes the church building for us will get the same reward I get if he remains faithful in his calling and position. Set yourself in order. We are not all apostles or prophets or workers of miracles (1 Cor. 12:28,29), but each of us has something to do. Whatever God has called you to do, do it. Set yourself in order.

4. God blesses your natural to be supernatural.

I love Proverbs 10:22, which says the blessing of the Lord makes rich and He adds no sorrow with it. God blesses your natural to be supernatural. Proverbs 10:22 actually is a double portion of blessing. That His blessing makes us rich is the first portion. The second portion is that He adds no sorrow with it.

Another word for *blessing* in the Old Testament is *favor*. Psalm 5:12 tells us of a supernatural blessing:

> **For thou, Lord, wilt bless the righteous; with favour wilt thou compass him as with a shield.**

That is God encompassing your life with favor.

That is God giving you favor with other people, God giving you favor on your job, God giving you favor when you go to buy a car or buy a home, God giving you favor in dealings with your relatives, and God giving you favor with your neighbors. God promised to shield your life with favor. God blesses your natural to be supernatural.

5. Think thanks.

Jesus took those five natural loaves and two fishes. He blessed them, and He gave thanks. Psalm 107:1 says to give thanks to the Lord, because He is good and His mercy endures forever. Many old songs in the Church, as well as a lot of David's psalms, are about giving thanks to God.

Every July, I preach at Brooklyn Tabernacle Deliverance Center in Brooklyn, New York. Under that big tent, the saints start shouting, and they all say, "Thank you." I bring that idea of thanks to God back home with me.

You may be in such a situation that you think, "What do I have to give thanks about?"

Here are some of the ordinary, routine things I give thanks for:

*I woke up this morning, thank you.

*I was able to get dressed by myself, thank you.

*I have food to eat and a cup of coffee to drink, thank you.

*I was able to get in a car and go to church on Sunday, thank you. I did not have to walk to church.

*I came into a nice church with heat and air and all the amenities, thank you.

Oftentimes, you get so caught up in what you do not have that you forget to give God thanks for what you do have. You ought to say thank you for what God's done in your life. *Think thanks.*

Second Timothy 3:2 describes a generation like this generation — unthankful, unholy, without natural affection. The more you do for this generation, the less it appreciates what is done and the more it demands. It is never satisfied and very seldom does it ever stop to say thank you.

God is good. God has been good. God will always be good. *Think thanks.*

6. God has a way to distribute your blessing.

Jesus blessed the loaves and blessed the fishes. He broke and distributed it to the disciples who distributed it to those who were "set in order." God has a way to distribute your blessing.

At one point in his life, Elijah the prophet was hiding by a brook, waiting out the three-year drought and famine God had brought on Israel because of Ahab and Jezebel. (1 Kings 17:3-9.) Twice a day, God sent ravens to Elijah with bread and meat. The Bible never says where the ravens came from, nor where the ravens got the bread and meat.

I do not know if they stole it. I do not know if they appropriated it in the name of the Lord. I do not know if God made a supernatural supply of bread and meat and commanded those ravens to take it to the prophet. I do not know how God made the ravens move contrary to their nature.

I only know that if you have a need, God has a way to distribute to that need. God has a way to bring the blessing about in your life, if you will just trust Him.

The Apostle Peter needed tax money, and Jesus said, "Go fishing." (Matt. 17:27.) He said, "Take the first fish you find, open its mouth, and inside, you will find a gold coin. Use that to pay your taxes." Peter followed instructions to the letter and was able to pay both his and Jesus' taxes. Peter was a natural fisherman who touched the supernatural.

7. Gather up the fragments.

Do not lose what God gives you. If God blessed once, He will bless again. When E.V. Hill, the nationally known pastor of a church in the Los Angeles area, spoke to one group of ministers, I was there. He said that, in some denominations, they make a real issue out of appreciation of pastors. Each year they have a pastor's appreciation service. All year long they raise money for pastor appreciation.

Oftentimes, pastor appreciation can be quite substantial. A friend of mine preached a pastor's appreciation in a major city. The pastor's appreciation offering was $250,000. After the pastor's appreciation, the deacon board in the church brought a gift of its own. They handed the pastor keys to a Mercedes 560.

E.V. Hill said, "Brethren, when you get that big pastor's appreciation offering, instead of going out and buying a Mercedes to impress all of the brethren, you ought to buy yourself some apartments" (as an investment).

I thought, "Right on! That is wisdom. The day may come when you are not appreciated as a pastor. The Mercedes, as fine a car as it is, may rust."

People have the mentality that God blessed me once, He will bless me again. That is true in principle. However, I discovered that, oftentimes, the reason people are in dire straits is because God *has* blessed them. And, instead of using wisdom in the blessing, instead of gathering up the fragments that nothing be lost, they left the fragments on the ground for the birds to devour.

It is only wisdom to exercise good stewardship as a believer. If you want to live supernatural living, gather up the fragments. When God gives you something, do not lose or waste any of it.

There has to be some significance to the two fishes and five loaves. The early Church in its time of hiding from persecution recognized one another by the sign of a fish. The Church still uses the sign of the fish as a symbol. You have probably driven down the road and seen a fish bumper sticker, or a sticker with a fish emblem on it.

In the Latin language, the word *fish* was an acronym (a word made of the first letters of other words) for the Latin words, "Jesus Christ, God's own Son, Savior." So early Christians made a play on words by using *FISH* as a hidden way of saying Jesus.

The two fish are symbolic, or types, also of how you are brought to Christ. You are born again, brought to God by the Word of God. (John 1:1, 14:23.) The first "fish" is representative of the Word. The second fish that brings you to Christ is the Holy Spirit. The Word and the Spirit bring us to Christ.

But what about the five loaves? What do the five loaves represent? Read Ephesians 4:11,12, where we are told that Jesus set in His Body apostles, prophets, teachers, evangelists, and pastors. He put the five-fold ministry in the midst of the Body to perfect us to do the work of the ministry.

The disciples were used by Jesus to distribute the five loaves of bread to those who were set in order that they might partake of supernatural living. That is why the Bible said in Hebrews 13:7:

> **Remember them which have the rule over you, who have spoken unto you the word of God: whose faith follow, considering the end of their conversation.**

I watched a talk show not long ago that really disturbed me. I watch them very seldom, and I do not believe three-fourths of what I do see. In fact, I wonder most of the time where they get these people from. On this particular talk show, three women claimed their pastors took sexual advantage of them.

They alleged their pastors were able to give them some really spiritual reasons why God said it was okay. Now I reserve judgment about anybody's credibility, but this truly disturbed me.

There are two principles in Hebrews 13:7 that you need to understand. First, remember them who have the rule over you if:

1. They have spoken the Word of God over you. (That means from the Bible, not some stretched or warped interpretation of their own.)

2. If their faith follows their *conversation*, which in King James' time meant what we would call "lifestyle." The original Greek word translated *conversation* is *anastrophe*, which literally means "behavior."[1]

Setting your life in order partly by submitting to the church authorities does not mean that, when you walk into a church, you are supposed to check your brain at the door!

If you see someone is claiming spiritual authority and leadership, see if that person's life is measuring up. See if the lifestyle is a lifestyle that you know to be in line with the Word of God and one that you would want to follow as a Christian.

Those three women said, "But they had such power."

It seemed to me that, instead of the pastors having power, the women lacked brains! They were like the nine hundred people who committed mass suicide in Jonestown, Guyana, in 1978 because one man said God told him to have them kill themselves.

Trust me on this, if I had been in that group, I would have been looking for a door. And if there had not been a door, I would have made a door somewhere. Actually, if those people had known the Word of God and tested Jim Jones' lifestyle, they would have been out of there long before things got to that stage.

It is no mistake that the typology for the five-fold ministry is five barley loaves. Barley was a peasant bread. It was also a leavened bread. Anyone looking for a perfect pastor or a perfect minister is going to look a long way because there are not any.

James advised that not many of the brethren be teachers, because those who presume to teach others are held to greater accountability. (James 3:1.) I talk to people all of the time who say they want to be in the ministry.

I tell them, "I will pray for you then. You will not only be judged by God, you'll be judged by the world, and more than that, you'll be judged by the Church."

You see, the burden of the ministry in 2 Corinthians 4:7, which says we have the treasure of Jesus in "earthen vessels" so that it might be obvious that the excellence of the power is of God, not us. The Treasure is still in earthen vessels.

When I was finishing this book, I wanted to be sure that this "earthen vessel" had made the points shown me by the Holy Spirit very clear to the reader, particularly in the conclusion. So I asked my wife for her input.

After more than twenty years of marriage, Connie and I think so much alike that sometimes it is scary.

I pressed my head up against her forehead one day, and she asked, "What are you doing?"

I said, "The Vulcan mind-meld," (a concept from *Star Trek* involving Spock's people).

However, we really do not need that because we think a lot alike; however, she very seldom gives me advice as to what I preach. She did give me her words of wisdom on the conclusion of *Order Out of Chaos*. Connie told me the conclusion ought to be really funny or really dynamic.

That put me on a spot, because I am not certain the conclusion is going to be really funny or dynamic. However, I sincerely pray this summation will help you understand the difference between God's order and the world's chaos.

Endnotes

[1] *Strong's*, "Greek Dictionary," p. 11, #391.

Conclusion:
The Choice Is Yours

I want to close this teaching with a story for an example, which we find in 2 Kings 7. However, first let us review Genesis 1:1. We saw in the first chapter of this book and in the Bible's "book of beginnings" that the earth, although created perfect and in order, had somehow become without form and empty.

We talked about why that happened, although we are not told much about it specifically in the Word, just an allusion here and there. Plus, what we are told and shown about God Himself makes it unimaginable that anything He created could be less than perfect.

The earth was in chaos when God began to re-create it in His six days of "labor" detailed in Genesis 1. As this is not a book on creation, but a book on spiritual order and chaos, we need to see the spiritual principles illustrated by the natural ones.

There is a parallel between the creation of the heaven and the earth and our lives. People have chaotic lives, and when the Spirit of the Lord begins to make new creatures (2 Cor. 5:17) out of those who desire to be "born anew," or born again (John 3:16), the Word of the Lord is heard — and out of chaos, there comes order.

God made man to exercise dominion (rule) over His creation. God made you to exercise dominion over your world. God gave you the authority to bring order out of chaos. God placed Adam and Eve in a garden of perfection, and they transgressed the law of God. Sin (chaos) entered into the world, but that did not change the plan of God.

Paul made it clear that there are only two races in God's order and exactly who was the head, or founder, of each race in 1 Corinthians 15:45,47:

> **And so it is written, The first man Adam was made a living soul; the last Adam was made a quickening spirit.**
>
> **The first man is of the earth, earthy: the second man is the Lord from heaven.**

That makes it very plain that the "first man," head of the "Adamic," unsaved, natural race was Adam, who let chaos into the world through allowing Satan to usurp dominion (over the world order, society, not over the planet). Paul said that *Jesus, the Second Man,* is also the "second Adam." That means He is the second Head of a race.

Everyone born naturally is descended equally from Adam and is part of the first race.

Everyone born of the Spirit is descended from Abraham and God through Jesus, the Head of our race, the second and last race.

Most Christians do not realize that, as believers, they are in a far better position than the first Adam.

A woman said to me once that she wished she had been with Adam in the Garden of Eden. She would have made certain they did not eat of that apple.

I thought, "Well, you're in a far better position than Adam was."

*Adam was a son by creation. You and I are born the sons and daughters of God.

*Adam talked with God in the cool of the evening and communed with God. You and I are filled with the Spirit of God. We have God *within* us, part of us, not just walking with us.

*Adam, as a "living soul" was led by his soul, his senses (mind, emotions, and will). We can be led by the Spirit of God. (Rom. 8:14.)

*Adam and Eve had authority in the earth. You and I have been given authority in heaven and in earth. We are in a far superior position than Adam and Eve occupied, even prior to the fall, because of what Jesus has accomplished in our lives. Are you glad for what Jesus did?

Having reviewed that foundation for how order became chaos, and what God did to restore order out of chaos, let us look at 2 Kings 6-8, where the city of Samaria, then the capital of the nation of Israel, was surrounded by the Syrian army.

An Example of How Chaos Brings Death

Things had gotten so bad under this siege that they were starving. There was cannibalism. People were even eating their babies. They were eating doves' dung and donkeys' heads.

The king only a short time before had seen the city receive a miraculous deliverance from Syria. (2 Kings 6:15-22.) Now, he was mad at God over the new Syrian siege. (2 Kings 6:30-33.) He looked for supernatural signs instead of supernatural living. And, as usually happens, he attempted to take out his anger at God on the servant of God. He sent someone to cut off Elisha's head. (2 Kings 6:31-33.)

Elisha, being a true prophet, knew the messenger from the king was coming to kill him. He was not afraid, nor did he retaliate. The Lord spoke salvation through him. He prophesied that the next day about the same time, fine flour and barley (the staples of life) would be sold cheaply at the gate of the city. (2 Kings 7:1.)

However, the king's officer was like the Israelites who scoffed at God providing food in the wilderness.

He said, "Hey, even if God opened literal windows in heaven, that could not happen!" (2 Kings 7:2.)

Before we go any further, let me tell you there are always going to be chaotic people around you. They are not going to believe the Word of the Lord, much less act on it. There are chaotic people who enjoy living from one crisis to another crisis to another crisis.

This Lord "on whose arm the king leaned" was one of those kind. Of course, the prophecy came true as did Elisha's rebuke to the doubter: "You will see it, but you will not eat any of it." (2 Kings 7:17-20.)

How God Used Chaotic People To Restore Order

Meantime, at the city gate were four leprous men. Lepers were not allowed to mix with "clean" people, but they could sit outside the gate and beg for help. Talking among themselves, they decided they were going to starve to death anyway, so they might as well go over to the Syrians and see if the soldiers would have pity and feed them. When they arrived at the camp, no one was there! (2 Kings 7:3-5.)

God had caused the Syrians to hear noises of troops marching on them. He had brought a delusion that many chariots, horses, and a great host of soldiers from the Hittites and Egyptians was upon them. They decided the king of Israel must have hired these soldiers to fight for him. So they fled in great fear and disarray. (2 Kings 7:6,7.)

The scene the four lepers came upon was scores of empty tents furnished just as they had been left, with food and drink in abundance, and horses and asses tethered nearby. As most of us would do, these lepers ran from one tent to another, eating something here and something else there.

They gathered up silver, gold, and clothes, and hid them. About that time, their consciences began to bother them as they thought of all the starving people in Samaria. They decided something bad would happen to them if they did not share the goodness of God with the rest of the people. (2 Kings 7:8.9.)

When the king first heard the report brought by the lepers, he thought that it must be a trap to entice them into opening the gates and coming out. So he sent spies, and the spies reported the lepers had told the truth. All of the Syrians' goods were there with not a soul to be found.

In fact, his spies followed the fleeing soldiers all the way to the Jordan River where they crossed to return to Syria. There were clothes and articles strewn all along the way, which the soldiers had discarded in their flight. (2 Kings 7:12-15.)

When the king announced to the starving people what had happened, they ran through the gates and trampled underfoot the man on whose arm the king leaned, fulfilling the word of the Prophet Elisha. (2 Kings 7:20.)

Keep in mind what we learned that *Elisha* means: Look who God used to bring about salvation: four leprous men in a chaotic condition. In leprosy (Hansen's Disease), the nerve system ceases to function properly. If they get burned, they cannot feel it. If they get cut, they do not feel it. When people have leprosy, particularly in advanced stages, they usually have lost some fingers or toes, or worse. They are literally falling apart. Their bodies are in chaos.

The four chaotic men sitting on the outside of the gate were in such dire circumstances that even the starving people did not want them in the city. However, they came out of chaos into order and saw the blessing of God. In the process, they became God's deliverers.

Five Steps That Will Establish Order

There are five steps these four leprous men took in becoming God's deliverers, five steps that brought them out of chaos and established the order of God in their midst.

1. They turned one to another and said, so we see that the first step involved their words.

God's first step in recreating this planet, in bringing order once again out of emptiness and formlessness was *words*. You may say, "Well, yes, but that is God." However, we saw that, as a Christian, you have the nature of God in you. You are born of "incorruptible seed." (1 Pet. 1:23.)

Just as "the Word was made flesh" (John 1:1) in Christ, the Word has been made flesh in you. You have God's nature as an inheritance from your Father, and God's nature is a creative nature. Paul wrote that we have the same spirit of faith: We believe and therefore we speak. (2 Cor. 4:13.)

You need to watch what you say because your words are creative words.

You need to watch what you say because your words carry authority. In Matthew 18:18, Jesus said:

> Verily I say unto you, Whatsoever ye shall bind on earth shall be bound in heaven: and whatsoever ye shall loose on earth shall be loosed in heaven.

Notice that Jesus did not say anything about you praying. He did not say anything about you invoking the Father. He did not say anything about you exercising the authority that is invested in His name. He simply said that "whatsoever" *you* bind or loose on earth shall be bound or loosed in heaven.

One reason many Christians find themselves in predicaments is that they keep speaking negative things into their lives, and negative things happen. Then they throw their hands in the air and do not understand why "God is allowing all of this to come my way."

In the meantime, God is up in heaven throwing His hands in the air saying, "I do not understand why you are allowing all of these things to come your way."

Have you ever met a genuine hypochondriac? Someone who is sick all of the time? If you ask how these people are, they will tell you more than you want to know about their health! It seems they get over one thing and come down with another. Why? Because they allow it. I used to think it was "all in their heads." But it is not; it is not in their heads, but in their hearts.

What they have allowed by their words is being allowed by God. You see, that is how dominion and authority are exercised. The Roman centurion who understood authority, also understood that authority is exercised through the spoken word. He knew Jesus only had to "speak the word" for his servant to be healed.

Watch what you say, because the Bible says that you are snared by the words of your mouth. You are taken captive by the words of your mouth. Jesus said in Matthew 12:37 that you are justified or condemned by your words. The beginning of action is in your words. Keep positive words.

2. The second step is *will*.

The four lepers arose, having said they would go to the Syrian camp. There is an act of the will involved. It is not enough to have words.

If you had met the Apostle Paul in the flesh, I am sure there was one overwhelming characteristic you would have noted in him. He was a very strong-willed man, before he was converted and after. You might even say that he was hardheaded. When Paul made up his mind, only God could change it.

There is power in a made-up mind. God has called us to exercise our wills. Many of you were taught to pray "not my will, but thine be done." However, the only times you can pray that is when you do not know God's will or when God lays something on you that is too much for you.

When Jesus prayed "not My will" in the Garden of Gethsemane, He saw what was ahead of Him. He wanted to make certain there was no other way mankind could be redeemed except by Him going to the cross.

Do you know how to know the will of God for your life? Get in the Word of God. If you get in the Word of

God, you will know the will of God. Philippians 2:13 says that it is God Who works in us "to will and to do His good pleasure."

The psalmist said that if we delighted ourselves in the Lord, He would give us the desires of our hearts. That does not mean that, if we "delight" in Him, He gives us whatever we want. It means that He puts the right desires in our hearts so that we want the right things, according to His will. If you want to set your will under the authority of the Holy Spirit, and you do not have a direct Word from God, do whatever is in your heart.

The lepers said, "If we go back into the city, we're going to die. If we sit here, we're going to die. But, if we move forward, we might live."

They had a will to do something. James wrote that faith without works is dead. (James 2:17.) Speaking without doing is useless. You are not going to come out of chaos until you do something. Oftentimes, people confuse their wishes with their wills. The difference between wishing something would happen and willing something to happen is called "want to."

Hosea 12:3, speaking about Jacob, said that he took his twin brother, Esau, by the heel while they were still in Rebekah's womb, and by his strength, Jacob had power with God.

Something in that child about to be delivered into this world said, "I'm going to be preeminent. I am a person of significance. The hand of God is upon me."

There was a "want to," even before he was born. How much "want to" do you have in your life? Do you have tenacity? Tenacity is when you have such a will toward God that you know the will of God, and you know the Word of God. You have purposed in your heart that you are going to tenaciously hold on to the will and the Word of God. You have purposed to do whatever it takes to see the will of God and the Word of God fulfilled in your life.

There is something about the people of God that I have never understood. Why is it that, when Christians get "between a rock and a hard place" or "where the rubber meets the road" — a place where circumstances and situations are going adversely — the first thing they do is quit praying?

The second thing they do is quit reading the Word of God. The third thing they do is quit attending church, and the fourth thing they do is quit paying tithes. Why is that?

You see, if I am sick and oppressed in my body, I am going to spend more time praying, reading the Word, and fellowshipping with the people of God. I am going to make certain that I pay my tithes, because Malachi 3:10,11 says that, if I do, God will rebuke the devourer for my sake.

If I am oppressed in my mind struggling with depression, I am not going to sit in front of the television and watch talk shows, soap operas, or violent movies.

If I am oppressed in my mind, or if I am weary in my mind, I am going to turn off television and read a good Christian book. I am going to fellowship with some good Christian people. I am going to read my Bible. I am going to meditate on the Lord. I am going to listen to some good Gospel music. I am going to turn off the rock and roll, the rap, the country and western music, and everything else.

I am going to wait on God. If I have a problem in my mind, I am going to put the right stuff in my mind. I think the problem is that a lot of folks do not have the "want to."

Every person can succeed in life. You will succeed at your own level, but every person can succeed. We have become a nation of "victims," people who come up with every excuse in the world for their lack of success. But the truth is, every Christian can succeed in life at his or her own level.

All you have to do is get God on your side.

All you have to do to get God on your side is to apply His Word to your life.

All you have to do is to come out of chaos into order, and you will succeed at your own level of life. You do not have to be a victim, but you have to have the "want to." Do you have the "want to"? Are you willing to walk out of chaos?

3. The third word is *walk*. The four lepers rose up to go. The Bible has a lot to say about your walk. Colossians 1:10 tells us to "walk worthy of the Lord."

How does a Christian walk worthy of the Lord? There are two qualifications in Colossians 1:10 that define walking worthy: 1) You are fruitful in every good work, and 2) you are increasing in the knowledge of God.

Let me tell you something about walking worthy with the Lord. It is a long walk. Every evening when it was nice, Connie and I used to walk through our neighborhood with our dogs. Halfway through the walk, one of us had to pick up our nine-year-old, decrepit little poodle and carry her.

I am sure our neighbors said, "Look at those funny people. One's carrying a dog."

Have you ever been on a long walk? A long walk is when you are walking somewhere, and when you get there, you are too tired to go home. For the last half of the walk home, all you can keep in your mind is one foot in front of the other. Your knees and feet are hurting. Your leg muscles are cramping, and all you can think of is one more step.

Christianity is a long walk. If you are not willing to walk the long walk, you are going to fail somewhere along the way. There are three sets of words to deal with: order and steadfastness, rooted and established, abounding and thanksgiving.

Your walk with God has to be an orderly walk. If it is, then your walk with God will be a steadfast walk. You will not be up one day and down the next day.

God has called you to walk in order with steadfastness, rooted, and established so that you can abound with thanksgiving. God meets you in your circumstances.

It has not been an instantaneous thing in my life, such as winning a sweepstakes, but it has been a progressive thing. God has moved me from glory to glory to glory to glory by His Spirit. That is a long walk. If you are walking that long walk, an orderly, steadfast, rooted, established walk, you will abound with thanksgiving. You will be blessed even when God blesses others.

4. The fourth thing the lepers did was *work*. When they got to the camp, they went into tent after tent and carried away silver, gold, clothes and other things. Then they hid those things.

Do you want to come out of chaos and walk in order? *Work.* If you are retired or planning on retiring soon, when you do, find something else to do. Do not give up and sit around the house doing nothing. Find something to do. If you have nothing else to do, go to church. If you do not need to make money, volunteer to help out wherever you can.

God never planned on anybody ever retiring. There is something you need to know about work: It develops character. (1 Thess. 4:11,12.) There is something about getting up in the morning and going to work. It is wonderful. If you do not enjoy what you are doing, start taking the necessary steps to get into a field you do enjoy.

The bottom line is, whether you like work or not, you need to work because that is God's plan. Work develops character. Work brings stability. Work also brings a sense of worth and a sense of purpose. Find something to do. If you are unemployed, find a job. In the meantime, your "job" is finding a job, and it starts at 8 a.m. every day. Work.

If you find yourself in poor circumstances, do not be afraid or ashamed of being poor, especially if you are doing everything you can do with what you have got. Keep believing, and you will see the blessing of God manifested in your life. God's plan works.

The four lepers went out and gathered spoils, and they hid them, which brings me to the last step they took in coming out of chaos into order and establishing order in the midst of the land.

5. They hid the gold and the silver. Before they told anyone else the Syrians had run away, they hid the gold and the silver. They did not want them in the city.

In fact, if you read that account carefully, you will find that after they went to the city gate and gave their news, they are never mentioned again.

The people in the city did not care about those four leprous men. They did not raise them on their shoulders as heros. They were lepers. Those four leprous men knew that, so they exercised wisdom.

Look at what Jesus said about wisdom in Matthew 11:19: **Wisdom is justified of her children.** And in Matthew 10:16: **Behold, I send you forth as sheep in the midst of wolves: be ye therefore wise as serpents, and harmless as doves.**

Jesus said, "Be like 'a sneaky snake.' Get wisdom. Get understanding."

After the people of Samaria had rushed out of the city to strip the camp clean, the four leprous men were left in the dust. Everyone else was gone.

I think one leprous man looked at the other leprous men and said, "It's time to go dig up our treasure."

The Bible does not tell us what happened to the four leprous men. God may have healed them because of their concern for the city. They could have run the other way. The Bible does not say. But, I believe those four grew to be really old, very rich lepers.

Order had come to their lives. They were never hungry again. You see, God wants to bring order to your life. When order comes into your life, there is blessing.

Some of you reading this book have no real order to your life. You need to make a choice, a choice to serve the Lord, a commitment to take the long walk to follow

Christ. God is saying, "Turn around. It is time to walk in the right direction."

Let me challenge you to make the right choices, ones that will bring about meaningful changes in your life. Then God will bring order from the chaos of life.